Being a Well Body of Believers

2nd Edition (6x9)

I0156385

By

Dr. Elizabeth A. James

FM Publishing Company
Cherokee, NC 28719

Being a Well Body of Believers, 2nd Edition (6x9)

Unless otherwise indicated, all Scripture quotations are taken from The New King James Version. Copyright ©1982, Thomas Nelson, Inc. Publishers. Used by permission.

Being A Well Body of Believers, 2nd Edition

Copyright © 2005 by E.A. James

FM Publishing Co.

P.O. Box 215

Cherokee, NC 28719

Printed in the United States of America

ISBN 9781931671262

Library of Congress Control Number 2011924082

Table of Contents

Introduction

Spiritual health and well-being are sometimes compromised at the expense of our struggle to attain physical health. Although both are important, our physical bodies are temporal. This book is intended as a self-help and self-monitoring tool for our spiritual condition.

The "30-for-30" spiritual well-being test is designed as a diagnostic tool to gauge how well we are doing in serving God and our fellow man. The health plan and prescriptions are from the Word of God to put us back on track before and after we allow ourselves to become ill and keep well fed to prevent us from "falling off track."

This book is a labor of love and concern for the body of Christ, the church. I've noticed, over my many years as a member of several bodies and in the ministry, that we tend to forget we are one body, one organism, and represent many members and parts, as the apostle Paul stated to the churches in Corinth, Ephesus, and in Rome. I have taken Paul's analogy a step further to help readers understand interdependence and inner workings of the natural body as it relates to the spiritual body, the body of Christ. I encourage readers to explore these inner workings and then answer individually for themselves:

How do I measure up spiritually?

Chapter 1. A Living Soul

"And the Lord God formed man of the dust of the ground and breathed into his nostrils the breath of life, and man became a living soul." (Genesis 2:7, LIB:KJV)

What does it mean to say God created man in His own image? From a human point of view, we tend to speculate on what God must look like. Prejudice and racism abound within churches. Many of European descent firmly believe that Jesus was blonde-haired and blue-eyed and since he is God's son, God must also possess these physical attributes. In contrast, many of African-American descent believe and affirm that Jesus had to be dark-skinned because he lived in the region close to Egypt, and also because the Bible says He had "hair of wool." Of course, this is the way the Apostle John described Christ during John's revelatory vision on the Isle of Patmos. Also, many of other races, ethnicities, and nationalities tend to reject Christianity altogether and opt for a religion of a faceless God, even to the point of calling themselves "gods."

People say "image is everything." What you believe about yourself governs your attitude towards life and will reflect itself in your behavior. People use image to sell products, usually to the point where the manufacturer is identified with the product. Case in point – we usually ask for a "kleenex" when we want a tissue. Although Kleenex is only one of the manufacturers of tissue, the company has become synonymous with tissue. In fact, while writing this book, I needed lower case for "kleenex" and my computer program (set for auto format) automatically changed the word to "Kleenex" with a capital "K." Another example is Levis. Although Levi is only one manufacturer of jeans, Levi has become synonymous with jeans. The general public, the consumers, have engrafted this into their psyches.

Is this the result of years of advertising or just plain good marketing? I believe it is both. Time is the issue. Both Kleenex and Levi have withstood the test of time. Their images stand tantamount to other manufacturers of the same products. They are accepted, trusted, and relied upon. God, even more so. God is synonymous with love, His greatest and best-selling product – all wrapped up in His son, Jesus. Therefore, Jesus is the image of God. He has withstood the test of time. He can and will always be trusted and relied upon to those of us who have "tried" Him. Many have accepted Him. However, God will not be satisfied until his marketing campaign is worldwide and widespread to the ends of the earth. He is patient and ever-merciful, not wanting anyone to perish. More importantly, God wants to recreate this image in the hearts and minds of every man, woman, and child.

Of course, like any good salesperson, God knew He would have to identify with his prospective customers. He would have to let them know He understands their plight. He knows their needs. And what's more, He has the answer to those needs. Therefore, Jesus found himself in the form of a man and humbled himself unto death on the cross (Phil. 2:8).

Every thought, temptation, trial, and test that we have or will ever encounter, Jesus has identified with and overcome. He showed us a more excellent way. His goal was to show us the true image of God, to offer himself as a sacrifice for our sins and give us hope and assurance that we too can become like him and weather through any and all trials. And lastly, he showed us that we can have eternal life and that the living soul God created can live on.

But, how does God do this? Since we understand that image is everything and we govern our lives by how things, places, and people are perceived, and since others judge us by how we are perceived, we need to understand how God sees us. God looks on the heart, that is, the internal, while man looks on the external. However, God made both internal and external. There is nothing made that was not made by Him (John 1:3). Man was formed of the dust of the ground, which means man contains, as biologists will attest, those basic elements within himself which can be found in the elements of earth, fire, and water. God breathed into us His life, and we became a living soul. We are first and foremost a soul with an outer layer of spirit and an outermost layer of flesh. Had God not breathed into us, we would not be physically alive.

Just like anything that has layers, you must peel away the top layers to get to the innermost layer. Every layer serves a purpose and cannot be discounted as useless. What God is most concerned with is our soul. Man is flesh and blood but God is also spirit. What happens to and within the outer layers greatly affects this delicate, precious, inner layer – the soul. These layers work under and are subject to different principles. That is, what is good for the flesh may or may not be good for the spirit and vice-versa. Ergo, the scripture "the spirit indeed is willing but the flesh is weak" (Matt. 26:41). What you put in your flesh can greatly affect, even kill the spiritual layers, and what you put in your spirit can greatly affect, even kill, the fleshly layers. Paul says these two are always at "war within our members" (Gal. 5:16-17).

However, they both have their growth process and timing. The Bible says "to everything there is a season and a time to every purpose under heaven" (Eccles. 3:1). All layers are growing as time goes on, that is, in a healthy normal body. When the flesh reaches its maturity, it begins to die. The spirit will continue its growth, if allowed to, and is not stunted. This growth continues until it outgrows the physical body and the spirit cannot and will no longer be contained in this "inferior" house. Paul says "to be absent from the body is to be present with the Lord" (2 Cor. 5:8). And the Bible also says that once man dies, the spirit returns to the Lord who gave it. But we are also told in the second book of Thessalonians that the "corruptible longs to put on incorruptible," and mortality longs to put on immortality (1 Cor. 15:53). We will receive a "heavenly body" like Christ when He appeared to his disciples before His ascension.

God has made it so that before the fleshly body is shed, the future of the soul is determined. Where will we spend eternity? Shall it be in the new heavens and new earth that God will create at the close of the millennium, or in the Lake of Fire, originally reserved for the Devil and his angels? It is the opinion of this author, not fact, that our next step once we are in God's realm at the close of the millennium, there will be another process of shedding the spirit layer. Please keep in mind that this is pure speculation and not something God has specifically revealed to me. It is not meant for man to understand all at this time, nor can we really understand all that God is doing or will do. Our minds are finite and limited in scope. I believe many have ventured into realms that God never intended, and have ended up destroying themselves in the process. The only thing of which we can be certain is that man is a living soul – composed of body, soul, and spirit. And before we can understand how to maintain the health of these layers until their "appointed time," we must first understand God's systematic schematic, that is, His plan, process, and procedure.

Chapter 2. God's Systematic Schematic

"For as the body is one and has many members, but all the members of that one body, being many, are one body, so also is Christ."
(1 Corinthians 12:12, LIB:KJV)

The Church

In Scripture, God likens the human body, that is, the fleshly body, to the spiritual body, that is, His church. There are four biblical definitions of the church. It can mean Christians at all times and places – the mystical body of Christ. It can mean the interdependent ministering community of believers world-wide. It can mean Christians in a particular city or province. And lastly, it can mean a group of Christians meeting together regularly, that is, a local congregation.

In the New Testament (NT), the word for church is ekklesia, which means "called out assembly." The secular Greek eekklesia was a political but never a religious assembly. However, in the Greek Septuagint, which is the Greek translation of the Old Testament (OT), it is regularly used for the Hebrew q'ahal, "congregation; especially the Pentateuch" (five books written by Moses). As a NT theological concept, "church" describes a new community, called out in the Gospel and set apart to God.

The NT consistently portrays the church as persons, not as an institution and never as a building. In Acts and the Epistles, "church" refers 92 times to local or provincial assemblies of God's new community: "the church that meets at their house," the "church at Antioch," or "the Galatian churches" (Romans 16:5; Acts 13:1; 1 Cor. 16:1). Twenty more times, ekklesia speaks of the whole community of believers, as in the statement that Christ is "head over everything for the church, which is his body" (Ephesians 1:22, 23). In this case, the term represents all Christians of every time and place bound together in a universal spiritual union.

Nature of the Community

The New Testament uses three powerful images to help us understand the nature of the church as people in a community:

The Church as the Body of Christ (1 Cor. 12:12-31).

The Church as the Family of God (Ephes. 1:22; 4:1-16), and

The Church as God's Holy Temple (Col. 1:18).

We relate to Jesus Christ as our Living Head. We are living members of His body on earth. God gives us spiritual gifts. We are to be responsible to Christ, our Living Head, to use our spiritual gifts to build up one another and represent Christ in the world. As a result, we in the community grow towards maturity.

Believers relate to God as Father in a family and to other believers as brothers and sisters. As members of God's family love and care for each other, intimate fellowship develops, community members experience the love of God together, and witness to His transforming power to this world.

As a holy temple, believers are building stones, linked to the Holy Spirit, who uses them to construct God's edifice on earth. Each stone in the divine construction is to exercise his or her priesthood, helping the community and individuals to grow in holiness.

Therefore God likens the human body to the spiritual body of His church, mainly because the spiritual body makes up all the components of, and is embodied in His son, Jesus Christ, who gave His life, His body, and His blood for us. This being the case, God has given us everything we need not only to examine and fully know the inner workings of the church body, but also to gauge the health and condition of the church body.

God is a God of order and does nothing randomly and in confusion or chaos. However, it should be noted that because of our finite minds, what may seem like chaos to us at times, is just another orderly way God is working. So, we should be led by His Spirit and led by His word when determining what is or is not "in order."

Our bodies were not just haphazardly thrown together. We serve a smart, powerful, all-knowing, and ever-present God. He knows the ending before the beginning. Why? Because He is Creator of all. A careful study of the human body reveals that we are made of tissue, blood, and bones.

There are eight systems - skeleton, muscles, circulatory and respiratory, digestive, urinary, glandular, skin, and nervous system. In order for these to maintain life, however, they must go through a process of recycling. We need to take in oxygen (O_2) and given off carbon dioxide (CO_2), that is, we need to take in oxygen because our tiny components, the cells within us, need this element to sustain them. We are made up of cells and to go even deeper, we're made up of tiny particles. Scientists have discovered these mysteries and are still delving into and searching the mysteries of life. However, no matter how much they search and how many discoveries they make, as long as they leave God, His son Jesus Christ, and God's Holy Spirit, out of the equation, they will be "ever learning and never able to come into the knowledge of the truth" (2 Tim. 3:7). God says that He takes the "foolishness of preaching" and it "confounds the [so-called] wise" (1 Cor. 1:18).

Scientists often try to use evidence in nature and proof of science to disprove the existence of God. However, there is more evidence in both nature and science that testifies to a higher being, an intelligent Creator who carefully planned and constructed this world from beginning to end. For example, Jason Ocker, in an article, states:

> "Not only was Geometry not invented by man, it was not developed by nature. Geometry neither exists in nature, nor does it have a physical existence (although it does have physical applications, such as the construction of bridges and skyscrapers, and computing orbits and vectors, but these constructs are not Geometry themselves, they are merely made possible because of its principles). One has to scour nature, in fact, to even find a semblance of approximate geometric shape. As Mandelbrot once stated, 'Mountains are not cones, clouds are not spheres, trees are not cylinders, neither does lightning travel in a straight line. Almost everything around us is non-Euclidean.'"
>
> Ocker goes on to say:

"Not only could Geometry be seen as a proof of Truth, one could go so far even as to say that it is a proof of God himself, or at least of a Creator. When one looks around at nature, one can conceivably see how chance might have arranged it. After all, as stated before, there is nothing so irregular as nature, the shape of trees and rocks are not precise at all, and one need only a topographical map to see a complete irregularity in the shape of forests and land masses and bodies of water. The details and workings of this planet do not happen like clockwork. Rain showers are not so timely as to be predictable, nor does the temperature alter consistently day by day. And yet, the idea of random processes which many use to explain the existence of nature could never be used to explain, as already shown, the utter and palpable existence of Geometry. In fact, I would even say that Geometry is a better proof of God than any 7 holy books and 3 modern prophets combined."

Although Ocker thinks Geometry is a "better proof," the Bible as a whole with the testimony of the prophets and Christ, Himself, do give an absolute proof of God, His nature, His purpose, His plan, and His systematic schematic.

As we examine the human body, its system and components, and its functions, we will see what spiritual truths and insights we can glean from it about the church body.

Parts of the Body

The body is made up of the head, neck, shoulders, arms, hands, back, front, lower section, hips, thighs, legs, and feet. These are the 12 major components. Although we will examine the inner-workings and functioning later, for now we will look at these specific parts.

These parts can be likened to or represented in the old dispensation, the 12 tribes of Israel, starting with Rueben, the firstborn, representing the head, and going down in succession as they were born, to Benjamin, the last born, representing the feet. Jacob loved every one of his sons, those born by Leah as well as those born by Rachel. They all fit together perfectly to form one close-knit family. However, if one member is despised or resented, as was Joseph, the body cannot function as a perfect whole. Joseph actually represented the lower section – very delicate region of the body. At times it may seem that more care and time is given to this area, at which time the other members may become "envious." The cruel action of Joseph's brothers against him can be likened to "cutting off your nose to spite your face."

This same attitude and type of envies and jealousies prevail in the church today. A pastor may tend to give more attention and care to one member that desperately needs that temporary extra care and attention, and the other members may tend to become jealous, spiteful, and even vengeful. For example, especially if the member happens to be female, the members will tend to perpetuate and spread idle gossip that the member and the pastor are engaging in activities that they shouldn't. This is called backbiting. If we look at the actual words "back biting," this implies that one part of the body is doing intentional harm to another part of the body. That is, the teeth are performing a function on the flesh of the back area. In some cases, if left unchecked, this action can lead to that part of the body being totally "devoured."

The Bible says we are "many members of one body," and that the foot should not say because I am not the eye that I am unimportant. Each one has its own function and purpose. In like manner, every member of the body of Christ has his or her own function and purpose. This relates to each individual's specific calling, along with his or her special gifts, talents, and abilities. However, what some fail to realize, is that a part can be versatile and can be used in different ways. For example, the feet and toes were not meant for picking up things, handling items, combing the hair on the head, or even feeding the mouth. However, as in the case of a body born without arms or because of unfortunate circumstances where the arms and/or hands have been amputated, the feet and toes now have to perform the function that the hands and fingers were supposed to perform or originally performed. The body, born without arms or its accompanying appendages, although having to learn to use these alternate parts to function, has a somewhat advantage over the body that loses the arms later in its growth cycle. The body now has to, with great difficulty, overcome this "handicap," and persevere. Such "handicaps" are churches that lose their church secretary, ushers, deacons, other willing workers, or even pastor, for whatever reason. But since God is the master designer of the church body, He, in His infinite wisdom, always equips other members who can fill in for these absent members. The church may have to work under a handicap because these members are put under a strain, having to perform more than one function at a time; that is, just as the body without arms, not only has to use the feet to walk on, but must also reach for and handle items. And just as we admire the person with the handicapped body who manages to overcome this handicap and perform normally, so too, we admire the church body that can overcome its handicap and perform its intended function.

The Head of the Body

Why spend a separate section on the head of the body? Is it more important than the other parts? God is "no respecter of persons" (Acts 10:34). That is, He loves every part of the church body and not one over the other. However, He does hold those parts accountable that have more and greater responsibility. The head is the only part comprised of seven separate openings, windows, or doors, if you will. The head has two eyes, two ears, two nostrils, and one mouth. The first six take in information and the latter, the mouth, speaks out that which has traveled throughout the body and become a part of the body, because it has affected the mind and taken up residence within the heart. The Bible says that "out of the abundance of the heart the mouth speaks" (Matt. 12:34).

Within the church body, the eyes can be likened to the pastors who are the under-shepherds and watchmen. They are the porters who must guard the door to the sheep so that the wolf does not enter in unawares. The ears are the prophets, for they must listen and hear God to direct the people where to go and sometimes how to go. The nostrils are the apostles who are commissioned to seek out, that is "sniff out," that which is unsavory or to detect and report back that which is savory and tasteful. The mouth represents the preachers and teachers who speak out the word once it is given. They instruct and communicate. Because of the sensitivity and inner-workings of these components, we can see that at times members within the head can be and are able to exchange functions. For example, in the human body, one can "see" with the ears and nose, and one can "hear" with the eyes and nose. Also, the eyes, ears, and nose can be used to "speak," "instruct," or "communicate." Such is the nature of nonverbal communication. Body language is an excellent tool, without words. We use sign language where we make symbols to represent words and phrases. And our hands can write words or symbols that the eyes can take in and interpret to the other parts. So we can see that no one part is an "island" unto itself.

It should be noted that although the components of the head and the members of the body are able to exchange functions and perform functions that they were not necessarily intended, this does not mean that components or members should usurp a function when that function is already being vitally performed. For example, an individual who is called to be an apostle can, with time, learn to be a pastor. However, not all apostles should be pastors. One case in point is an individual who referred to himself as an apostle, did not adequately possess the qualities needed to be an effective pastor, such as patience, tender care, understanding, and humility. What is even more important is that this individual wanted to control and lead with an iron hand. He reminded me of King Saul who mercilessly persecuted and pursued David, who was to be Saul's successor. Out of rage and jealousy, Saul ended up destroying his own life and soul. He kept operating under the belief that he still had the anointing of God when it had been long withdrawn from him. So members should be careful in this area even if one knows his or her calling and that he or she possesses multiple gifts and callings. The Spirit of God will lead us into all truth in this area and all areas. He will let us know where we should be at all times, even if it does not "feel" comfortable. Our obedience is what matters.

All seven openings of the head also give out waste products. They are the sensors that inform the head of the body that something is wrong or that things are performing well. We know this because every time we go to the doctor for a checkup, the doctor checks our vital signs. He first looks at the overall condition, looking for changes or irregularities from either the norm, or if there is a recorded history, from what is normal for that specific body. The nurse will take the weight of the body to see if there is a significant loss or gain. More times than not when the body is sick, there is a significant weight loss, so, too, in the church body. When there is a significant decrease in church membership, this is a clue that something is amiss – either individually or wholly.

Just as the doctor will try to research and examine the causes of the weight loss, so too the pastor of the church may search for what led to the drastic and significant loss in membership.

The nurse will also take the body's temperature. Normal is considered between 98 to 99 degrees for warm-blooded bodies such as ours. The church's temperature should be pretty hot also. That is, the fire of the Holy Spirit should be continually burning throughout the church body, purifying and convicting, ridding itself of all unhealthy impurities and wastes within the system. Jesus said, "I know your works, that you are neither cold or hot. I wish you were cold or hot, because you are lukewarm I will spew you out of my mouth" (Rev. 3:15-16). A body whose temperature is lukewarm is considered too low and the body's life is in danger. So too it is with the church body. If the power of the Holy Ghost is not given reign and not allowed to heat it up to normal so that it can perform its reasonable service, it is not considered a healthy body and of course of no use.

Circulatory System

One of the last vital signs that the nurse will take is blood pressure. The life of the body is the blood. The blood is the life-sustaining fluid in the veins and arteries of humans and animals. The Bible treats blood (Hebrew, dam) as sacred fluid, symbolic of life, which is itself the gift of God. The thought is best expressed in Lev. 17:11: "The life of a creature is in the blood, and I have given it to you to make atonement for yourselves on the altar." Since blood represented a creature's life, the Jew was forbidden to drink blood or use it in foods (Deut. 12:23).

Most of the 360 OT occurrences of dam (blood) fall into one of two categories: (1) Blood denotes violence, either in lawful war or by murder. Usually the plural is used in such cases; it may be rendered "bloodshed" or even as "blood-guiltiness" in some passages, like Ps. 51:14. (2) Blood expresses the essence of the OT sacrifice, in which an animal substitute was killed to make atonement for human sins.

In the NT haima (blood) also often refers to bloodshed, and at times to OT sacrifices. But 38 of the NT's 99 uses of the term refer to the blood of Christ. The "blood of Christ" conveys two major theological emphases. (1) The death of Jesus on the cross is viewed as instituting the new covenant, which God promised through the OT prophets (Jer. 31:33,34). In OT times the sealing of a covenant by sacrifice, a "covenant of blood" (illustrated in Gen. 15:8-21), made it the most binding of OT commitments. As a "covenant of blood," Christ's death expresses God's total commitment to forgive all who believe in His Son. (2) But the "blood of Christ" is also viewed as the fulfillment of all that the OT sacrifices foreshadowed. The sinless Son of God gave His life that human beings might be redeemed (Eph. 1:7); He, Himself, because the sacrifice of atonement by which we have been reconciled to God. (RBD, 93)

The blood circulates throughout every artery of the body, that is, in a normal body. If the pressure is too high or too low there is an indication of either a problem in the heart or a problem that will have direct negative effects on the heart. If the pressure is too high, the possibility of a stroke ensues. In case of stroke, if death does not ensue, part of the body is left paralyzed and useless, and the head and its components can no longer perform with effectiveness nor with efficiency that which they were intended. If the pressure is too low, again there is an indication of a heart problem or a problem that will directly affect the heart. Not enough blood is being pumped through the system. Sometimes this is an indication of a blood clot. Low blood pressure can also be due to an inordinate amount of blood loss.

So, too, the church body's blood pressure needs to be adequately regulated. Just as in the human body where the life is in the blood, so too, within the church body, is life in the blood of Jesus who shed every drop on Calvary to pay the penalty for our sins. He left not one drop back. By his stripes we are healed (1 Peter 2:24). Jesus' sacrifice on the cross and

His resurrection is the whole basis of our faith. This blood must be continually and adequately flowing throughout the body of Christ, the church. The main arteries are: (1) exercising faith, (2) prayer, (3) fasting, and (4) studying the word of God. It is through these avenues that the blood of Jesus is transmitted throughout the body.

Exercising Faith

Faith is belief, confidence, trust, or reliance. In the Bible, religious faith is a life-shaping attitude toward God. The person with faith considers God's revelation of himself and of truth to be certain and sure. The person with faith then responds to God with trust, love, and obedience.

God made promises to Abraham, and the Bible says, "Abraham believed the Lord, and He [God] credited it to him as righteousness" (Gen. 15:6). God gave Israel a Law that revealed his moral character and guided the believer's faith-response (Deut. 4:5-8). In the NT, the object of faith is Jesus. Only 12 times does the NT speak of "faith in God" rather than faith in the Lord Jesus Christ, because Jesus is now the one in whom God has fully expressed himself.

Biblical faith, then, has two aspects: on God's part there is an act of revelation that calls for a response; on man's part there is a response of faith that evaluates God's revelation as trustworthy and responds wholeheartedly to the Lord. Thus, God presents Jesus as His Son, whose death wins us forgiveness, and we, by faith, rely completely on Jesus for our salvation.

But we must exercise our faith daily. Anything that is exercised on a consistent basis is built up stronger and stronger. Jesus said that with faith as a grain of a mustard seed, which is the smallest of all seeds, we could move mountains (Luke 17:6). Without faith it is impossible to please God, says apostle James (James 2:20). By faith, says Paul, Abraham, Moses, Rahab, and others were able to accomplish amazing Feats. They believed what God said. They had seen His miraculous works; they trusted God implicitly, and they activated their faith through action. Abraham moved out on faith when God told him to "get to another country" (Gen. 12:1). He was faced with venturing out in an unknown land. But when God said move, Abraham moved. Because of his obedience, God promised and God made good His promise, that Abraham would become the "father of all nations," and that Abraham's seed would be like the "stars in the sky" (Gen. 22:17) and like "the grains of sand" (Heb. 11:12). Abraham's faith was further tested, as our faith is, and he was told to offer up his only son through whom God said would come many nations. As far as we know, Abraham did not question God. He trusted God completely, without murmuring, without complaining. Abraham knew that if God had him offer up his only son that God was more than able to raise the child back from the dead. Abraham knew that his obedience was being tested.

Today, we must deal with skeptics who will read this account of Abraham with different reactions. Some feel that the story is not true. Some feel that this account has led to others being misguided, such as the man who beheaded his son because he said God told him the boy had a demon and must die. And there are others who believe the Bible, but have a hard time dealing with God requiring obedience to the point of requesting that Abraham sacrifice (that is, slay) his only son. To the first two groups – those who don't believe and those who believe that this account has misguided others – it should be noted that the Bible is true whether or not a person believes it. Also, in this dispensation, under the New Testament, God will not require a person to murder another human being. We understand and know that a person who is possessed by a demon must be delivered through effectual and fervent prayer by a righteous believer who has fasted beforehand. If that demon-possessed individual were just slain as in the case of the father beheading his son, that demon which is an evil spirit, will not be destroyed. We serve an intelligent God who knows and understands this. To the last group – those who believe yet feel uncomfortable and are unable to reconcile their ambivalence about God's seemingly unfair request of Abraham to sacrifice his only son, it should be noted that I used to feel this same way many years ago. I had heard about Jesus and thought only that He was an extremely good person. I could not believe nor understand why anyone would want to hurt and kill such a good person. In my eyes, he had done nothing wrong and certainly nothing worth dying for. I decided to read the Bible for myself. I was an avid reader and thought myself to be extremely intelligent. I felt that if I wanted to know what was in the Bible, what it was all about, and to understand it, all I had to do was read it from beginning to end – which is what I attempted to do. However, this portion of scripture dealing with God's request of Abraham was my one stumbling block. Every time I would get to this point in my reading I would stop, failing to understand how a just and holy God could do such a thing. I attempted to read the Bible, starting at the beginning on three separate occasions. I encountered the same stumbling block all three times.

Finally, I explained to one of my closest friends the problem I was having. "You're starting in the wrong place," he told me. "You have to first come to Jesus before you can get to God." He told me to start reading the New Testament; that is, read Matthew, Mark, Luke, John, and then all of the New Testament. Then, go back to the Old Testament and start at Genesis. By the time I finished the New Testament, I had given my life to Christ. When I got over to the Old Testament and read the entire story about God's request to Abraham to sacrifice his only son, when the angel told Abraham not to slay Isaac because Abraham had shown God that he was willing to give up all for Him, and the words "God will provide himself a lamb for a burnt offering" (Gen. 22:8), everything wonderfully clicked. I rejoiced in my spirit because now I understood. You see, God never asks us to do anything that He hasn't already done Himself. God, in the form of Jesus Christ, left His heavenly home and came down in the form of a man, humbled Himself and was obedient even to the point of death. When I realized that not only was Jesus – God, but that this same God loved me so much that He gave His life – every drop of His blood for me.

Another great and momentous example of exercising one's faith is in Moses. The Bible says that:

> "By faith Moses, when he had grown up, refused to be called the son of Pharaoh's daughter, choosing rather to endure ill-treatment with the people of God than to enjoy the passing pleasures of sin, considering the reproach of Christ greater riches than the treasures of Egypt; for he was looking to the reward. By faith he left Egypt, not fearing the wrath of the king; for he endured, as seeing Him who is unseen. By faith he kept the Passover and the sprinkling of the blood, so that he who destroyed the firstborn would not touch them" (Heb. 11:24-28).

Moses had everything as far as the world imagines: prestige, power, and prosperity. Yet by faith he followed a burning bush, a bush that burned right along with the burning desire to seek the answer to the great call that awaited him. He exercised his faith. It led him to God.

When a person is operating off the faith of others, he cannot last. He becomes sluggish, as the blood in the body becomes when it is filled with excess cholesterol. Cholesterol comes from fats in those good old sugary items we love to plunge into our bodies because they taste so good. People who are operating off the faith of others are getting the overflow, the desserts that taste so good. However, all fluff and no substance – one is unable to sustain itself because there is no foundation on which to stand. To make good blood, one must eat of the Bread of Life for oneself. This bread, once eaten daily, will break down into carbohydrates, which the body needs. This represents the sweet personal testimony of the believer. Now others can benefit from his or her overflow. It should be noted that the overflow is never a substitute for making good blood. At times we may need a transfusion. However, a good spiritual life cannot be sustained this way.

Prayer

The human body needs O_2, that is, Oxygen, in order to survive. We take air into our lungs and expel CO_2, Carbon Dioxide gas, which is used by trees and other plant life that utilize CO_2 and give off oxygen. God is a God of order and does nothing haphazardly as we stated earlier. Everything He created for us is a process of give and take. If we only took in oxygen and never gave out carbon dioxide, all the plant life and trees would die, and then consequently, so would we. So too, it is in the spiritual body (the church). Prayer is essential and can even be called "the breath of life." Each believer needs to have a constant and continual prayer life, and so does the church as a body. When we pray we talk to God. Sometimes our prayers are petitions. Sometimes they are intercessions for others. Sometimes they are lamentations. And other times we are just praising God and thanking Him for His love and kindness. Also, we should remember that God is not some impersonal, mysterious, unreachable being. God is three in one: God the Father, God the Son, and God the Holy Ghost. They are separate personalities with different functions, yet they agree as one. To get to God you must come by His Son, Jesus, but before you can get to Jesus, you must be convicted and drawn by the Holy Ghost. In prayer, the Holy Spirit takes your prayers to Jesus who comes before God with your prayers. Because this process is so fast, sure, and steady, it may not seem like it is taking place. When you have given your life to Christ and the Holy Ghost dwells within you, you make direct connection to God and with God. We become His sons, his children, and our Father is more than willing to give us the desires of our heart. Note that Scripture says we should ask "in the name of Jesus" (John 14:13-14). When we pray, God does not see our lowly, sinful lives. He sees the blood-washed righteousness of His Son, Jesus Christ.

When prayers are made for others within a church body, no one person will have to worry about his or her needs being met. For example, let's take Members A, B, and C.

Member A prays continually for Member B and Member B prays continually for Member C, and Member C prays continually for Member A. Everyone is taken care of. Each individual receives a dual blessing, the blessing received from the prayers of others, and more importantly, the blessing of giving out prayer for someone else other than oneself. Jesus said in the book of Luke that we should "give and it shall be given unto you, pressed down, shaken together, and running over, shall men give unto your bosom, for with the same measure that you mete withal, it shall be given unto you" (Luke 6:38). Jesus was referring to us receiving whatever we give out. In verse 37, He says "judge not lest ye be judged, condemn not, lest ye be condemned, forgive and ye shall be forgiven." Instead of being critical and finding fault with others, we should forgive them and pray for them. Most of the churches use verse 38 to refer to giving of our tithes and offerings. There is nothing wrong in and of itself with this application of the Word, but Jesus meant it in terms of giving of ourselves. And what better way to give of oneself than through prayer.

Judson Cornwall reminds us that the Bible is a prayer book. It commands us to pray (over 250 times), and it speaks of "prayer," "prayers," and "praying" another 280 times. We should be reminded that Adam and Eve had no Bible. They enjoyed direct communication and communion with God. Because of their disobedience, they no longer enjoyed this personal relationship with God. The sacrifice of Christ at Calvary was for more than provision for the forgiveness of sin. It was to restore men and women to personal communication and fellowship with the Father. Cornwall says, "Whereas prayer as a cry is usually a monologue, prayer as conversation must be a dialogue." (Praying the Scriptures: Communicating with God in his own Words by Judson Cornwall)

Fasting

Fasting is going without food and/or water or can also mean consuming only water and simple foods. Many biblical fasts lasted for a day, from sunrise to sunset; some continued for several days. Individuals often fasted when in the grip of some crisis or strong emotion (1 Sam. 1:3-7; 2 Sam. 12:15-18; Dan. 6:18). Old Testament Law legislated fasting only on the Day of Atonement (Lev. 16:29; Jer. 36:3). Public fasting was associated with national repentance (Neh. 9:1) and crisis (Judg. 20:26; 1 Sam. 7:6; 2 Chr. 20:3). These fasts were typically accompanied by confession and by earnest appeal to God in prayer.

When fasting expressed true repentance and grief, God responded with acts of deliverance (Jonah. 3:5-10; Esth. 4:3, 16; 9:31). At other times, however, fasting was little more than a hypocritical attempt to manipulate God. In the time of Isaiah, for example, the people complained that they had fasted, but God had not seemed to notice (Isa. 58:2,3).

Isaiah's response is significant. God cares more about righteousness than fasting. Obedience is better than sacrifice (1 Sam 15:22).

After 586 B.C., the destruction of Jerusalem was commemorated with four annual fasts, mentioned only in Zech. 7:1-7 and 8:19. Again, God questioned the motive for these fasts, saying that Israel fasted for them rather than for him. And again the Lord returned to the central issue: "Administer true justice; show mercy and compassion to one another. Do not oppress the widow or the fatherless, the alien or the poor. In your hearts do not think evil of each other" (Zech. 7:9-10).

Criticism of ritual fasting is also found in the NT. Jesus dismissed those who paraded their piety on the two traditional fast days, Tuesday and Thursday. On those days they looked somber, disfiguring their faces to make sure everyone knew they were fasting. Dryly, Jesus commented, "They have their reward" (Mt. 6:16-18).

Jesus criticized the misuse of fasting, not fasting itself. He himself fasted for 40 days before beginning his public ministry (Mt. 4:2), yet he noted that fasting was not appropriate for his disciples while he was present with them. Rather, it was a time for rejoicing (Mt. 9:14, 15; Luke. 5:33-35). The reference in Mk. 9:14-29 to fasting and prayer to cast out demons, like that in 1 Cor. 7:5 is not in the oldest Greek manuscripts and may be an addition to the original text. The NT Epistles contain no encouragement to fast.

Yet believers did fast in the apostolic age, when ordaining elders and teachers (Acts 13:2-3; 14:23) and occasionally in times of special need (compare Acts 12:5; Acts 27:1-38). Soon after the apostolic age, Christian leaders called for fasting before baptism, at Easter, and as a weekly habit on Wednesdays and Fridays.

It is clear that fasting is an appropriate expression of grief or deep religious need, but fasting is no substitute for a heartfelt commitment to righteousness and justice. Fasting is no meritorious act, nor a way to win a "more spiritual" rating from God or from others. Some Christians today fast as a spiritual discipline: to develop proper control over bodily desires or to prepare for a special task or decision. (RBD, 213)

Food for the Body

Now that the body is cleansed internally, it is ready for good food. What qualifies as good food is that which contains the necessary vitamins and minerals, that is, the necessary nutrients so that the body can generate and regenerate healthy life-giving cells. The body needs such vitamins as A, B-complex, C, D, E, and many others. It also needs minerals such as Magnesium, Potassium, and Zinc. Every one of these nutrients is what the body is already comprised of and what is contained within the environment in which the body lives. All we are doing is putting back into the body what is depleted throughout the day. Nutrients are utilized by the body to create energy so that the body is able to perform work. The body that does a lot of work, has expended a lot of energy, and therefore utilized a lot of nutrients. These nutrients must be put back either through the foods we eat or through supplemental man-made nutrients. More times than not, we need these artificial nutrients because we neglect to eat the right and necessary foods. And although these supplements may help us in the short term, they also harm in the long run because they contain fillers and additives for which the body has no use.

Of course, we know that within the church body, this good food is the Word of God. The Bible says to desire the "sincere milk of the word that you may grow thereby" (1 Peter 2:2). And as the body grows, it needs the proper "meat" of the word. It should be noted that during King James' day, the word "meat" did not necessarily refer to the flesh of animals. It meant simply "food" or nutrient. Many have heard the expression, "you are what you eat." This is absolutely true. If you feed yourself with candy and cakes but never put fruit, vegetables, protein from beans or meat, or nuts and grains into your system, you will no doubt develop a myriad of ailments, possibly sugar diabetes, a degenerative disease. We know that the best food is that which is pure and absent from insecticides, additives, or preservatives. The same is true for the Word of God. Our body must be fed the pure, unadulterated Word of God. It must be rightly divided and served so that it can be tasted, chewed, and thoroughly digested. If you swallow big portions whole you'll probably choke to death. But if it is broken down into bite sizes, one can partake of it daily. It can also be an enjoyable experience if you have anointed and experienced servers who are sensitive and Spirit-led teachers and preachers of the Word.

Sometimes we must eat vegetables such as broccoli or cauliflower that, unless one has acquired a taste for them, are not readily delectable to our pallets. However, they contain nutrients in higher quantity than most other foods. The Word we are served might not always be to our liking. Most people have "itchy ears" and only want to hear those things that sound good to them, those things that will make them feel good about themselves, and those things that will make them jump and shout. However, God sent meals through His servers (such as Isaiah, Jeremiah, and Ezekiel) that were so "bitter" even the servers did not like serving them. But God requires us to "eat the whole roll," not just what we like to hear.

There are some who may have enjoyed the meals previously, but may despise the server and therefore decide they will not enjoy any portion of the meal. We sometimes care too much about who the Word is coming through, their personality, what they are wearing, to whom they are related, and what they were like in the "old man," to the point that we miss a perfectly good nutritious meal. In fact, the body may have grown or been revived 10 times faster had it received this nutritious meal. Remember, the church body needs this nutrition of the Word of God so that its cells can utilize the proteins to make energy to do work. So, it's easy to tell when the church body is not getting the proper nutrition it needs. It will be doing very little work.

At times the church body will be getting a lot of the wrong foods and therefore its body cannot perform its required function. This leads to "spiritual fatness." The body has become lazy and lethargic and is taking in, but not giving out. When a church body is full of the Word but never witnesses, never takes the Word to a dying world, never shares it with those in need, the body risks heart attack, hypertension, and other ailments that will affect the life blood flow of the body. That system of give and take which God ordained is greatly curtailed. This fatty tissue exists because no energy was expended through work. God says we should present our bodies "as a living sacrifice" (Rom. 12:1). The work we do for God is our reasonable service. It shows when a church body has gone beyond this reasonable service. You have a church body that is finely-tuned, united, and full of power. They are mighty to pulling down of strongholds, and subduing every high thing that exalts itself above God. They are conquering spiritual demons such as fear, depression, anger, jealousy, and gossiping. This church body is going for the "gold," and can out-distance its opponent, the Devil. It can run faster than its enemy because it has forgotten "those things which are behind" and is pressing "toward the mark of the prize of the high calling of Christ Jesus" (Phil. 3:14). It knows that its body may have to suffer for a time, giving up the sacrifice of praise, and suffering for the name of Christ due to opposition of the world. But it knows that it will reach its goal if it just endures and persists, and will one day stand in reverential awe, with humility by Christ's righteousness, as all of Heaven sings the heavenly anthem, "Holy, holy, holy is the Lord of hosts" (Isaiah 6:3). For they know that all things shall pass away, but God's Word will stand forever. So they have partaken of it, digested it, and utilized it, so they can become what they eat.

Well of Water

Our physical bodies are made up of 75% H_2O, that is, water. The environment in which we live is made up of the majority of water. The Bible says that in the beginning the "world was void and without form" (Gen 1:1). This is how water is; it has no substantial shape or form so that we grab hold of it. The Bible says that God divided the waters from the waters. This shows His majesty and power, for He did it only by speaking the Word. Since we are made of majority of water, our bodies need water in abundance to survive. Most say that we should drink between 8 and 12 glasses of water a day – some say one-half of your body weight in ounces each day. This helps purify the system and helps the body reach its maximum performance. Each cell needs water because water creates the reservoir in which the cells can freely move to build its proteins. When we are thirsty, especially when it seems as if the heat has depleted every drop within us, nothing else will satisfy like a cold glass of water. A man who is in the desert with the hot sun beating upon him does not crave food. He does not want money, prestige, fame, or power. He craves water. The physical body is craving that which it knows is its life source, that which its body is comprised. It needs that life-giving water. The body can go longer without food than it can without water. Without water, the body will most assuredly die.

For the church body, this well of water is Jesus Christ. While we were yet sinners he died for us. He paid the price and bought us. We belong to him and are comprised of him, at least 75%. You see the other 25% are the tares and the sheep in wolves clothing – those who don't hear his voice because they are not called by his name. Much of this 75% of liquid is expended through the body and must be put back. Jesus told the Samaritan woman at the well that if she believed on him she would never thirst, but would have "a well springing up into everlasting life" (John 4:14). The well will never run dry because Christ will steadily replenish it.

He knows automatically how much we need, whether it's 8 glasses, 10, 12, or half our body weight in ounces daily. But we must be filled daily. Jesus accomplished this by sending The Holy Spirit who came in the name of Jesus. The Holy Spirit interprets our prayers and He knows when we're in the desert. He knows the direct road and will lead us to that life-giving water, Jesus. But we have to be willing to seek him. We have to be "thirsting after the Lord" (Matt. 5:6). Some are thirsty, but don't realize that it is Jesus they need. They are drinking sodas and eating candy bars and getting thirstier every day with no satisfaction. Whenever the physical body craves sweets it is usually because the body is thirsty for water. Sugar is tasty but will rot the mind and the teeth if taken in excess quantities for too long a period of time, eventually causing the body to degenerate. The person may not understand yet that this is what the body needs. It takes the conviction of the Holy Spirit to lead the body into "all truth" to the life-giving water.

Chapter 3. The Heart of the Matter

"A man's heart plans his way, but the Lord directs his steps."
(Prov. 16:9)

We've talked about the blood flow to, from, and through the heart, and what effects the flow can have on the heart. A body can live without several different parts of the body such as the appendix, one of its lungs, one of its kidneys, or even one or both of its other appendages like an arm or a leg. But a body cannot live without the heart. Spiritually, the heart represents the thoughts of the mind. "Out of the heart flows the issues of life" (Prov. 4:23). "Out of the abundance of the heart, the mouth speaks" (Matt. 12:34). The heart is the seat of where we live. One can see what is in the heart of the church by what it says, what it does, and how well what it says matches up with what it does. For if the walk does not match the talk, hypocrisy ensues.

The heart is the center of the church body. Just as the heart beats within the healthy natural body constantly and continually, so too, the spiritual heart should constantly and continually beat within the church body. This beat is the steady rhythm of righteous words matching up with righteous living. It is also the steady rhythm of a church body centered on its true purpose: to win souls for Christ.

There are several irregularities of heartbeats. There are heart murmurs; there are hearts that beat much slower than others; there are hearts that beat extremely fast. And, of course, there is the deadly heart problem that leads to a heart attack. The heart murmurs within the spiritual body represent the distinct and tell-tale signs of hypocrisy. A church body will use scripture to back up what it wants to do. For example, members are frequently reminded that we are under the "new dispensation," that is, the law of grace in the New Testament era. However, when it comes to tithes and offerings, the church will rely mostly on the verses in Malachi where we are told to bring the tithes and offerings into the storehouse and to not "rob" God (Mal. 3:8). If asked for a NT reference for this principle of tithing, most churches will resort to Luke 6:38: "Give and it shall be given unto you, pressed down, shaken together, and running over shall men give unto your bosom. For with the same measure that you mete withal, it shall be measured to you again." We know that there is only one interpretation of scripture; however, scripture can be applied in different ways. Although there is nothing wrong with applying this scripture in this case, it should be noted that Jesus was not talking about giving of money. If you start at the first verse of the chapter, Jesus says "judge not, lest ye be judged, condemn not, lest ye be condemned, forgive and ye shall be forgiven" (Luke 6:37). It is interesting that this part of scripture is never read before the other. So, taken out of context, one would only believe that he was referring to the giving of money. But in actuality, Jesus was talking about not judging, not criticizing others, but forgiving them, and giving of ourselves. He was saying that how we treat others is exactly what we will receive in return, that is, with the "same measure that we mete withal" it shall be measured to us again. But Jesus also says before this, that if you give of yourself for others and forgive, you will receive it back "pressed down, shaken together, and running over." It should be noted that members should give willingly and as they are led by God and should give in a cheerful manner. "God loves a cheerful giver" (2 Cor. 9:7).

In the natural body, a slow heartbeat usually occurs when the body is asleep. The same is true of the church body. A slow heart beat means the church is saying a lot of things, but doing very little, if nothing at all. It meets for services each week, sometimes several times a week. It preaches and teaches the word faithfully – to the same members and people who have been there for years and still haven't reacted or pro-acted on what they have heard or learned. A body that is asleep may feel that it is "steadfast, immovable, and always abounding in the word of the Lord" (1 Cor. 15:58). It may be fooled into thinking it is "rooted and grounded," when it is in reality lying dormant. When the body is asleep, its members and parts are unproductive. Its mind, that is, the head is in a dream state – that is, fooled by Satan that it is doing the will of God. The Bible says that the "very elect" would be practically fooled. In this state, the tiny cells within the body are steadily rejuvenating themselves. They are constantly working and building themselves up. However, these cells know that all is in vain if the body should never wake up. These tiny cells are those insignificant members within each local body who are actively witnessing, actively feeding the poor, teaching and preaching, walking in the word of God, and visiting and caring for those whom others seem to have forgotten. They are doing this without "blowing a trumpet" before them. They do their "alms in secret," and God "rewards them openly" (Matt. 6:1). They rarely, if ever, get recognition from man, that is, from the head. They don't crave any recognition and they don't have time to murmur, complain, backbite, or even worry about it, because they are constantly working by building up the spiritual church body, which is God's kingdom.

The fast heart beat represents the church body who is active, moving, and going forth. It is doing more than what it talks about. There are a few of these around. However, it should be noted that most of these are non-denominational in nature. Many churches that are denominational in nature tend to be so highly structured and organized – much like the government. This principle would work if it operated in the way it is supposed to work, just as the human body is structured and highly organized in nature. For example, the natural body (in general) is organized as follows:

1) Cell

2) Tissue

3) Organ or Part

4) System

5) Body

That is, there are five levels. The body was created first from a living cell. This cell multiplied and became tissue, which multiplied and became an organ. Many organs were created and function interdependently within their own systems. Each system cooperates interdependently with each other to form a complete healthy body. The nine systems can be compared with the fruit of the Holy Spirit.

Within the spiritual body, that is, the church, the same applies as in the natural body. There are five levels:

1) local members

2) district members

3) state members

4) regional members

5) national members

International was not included because this would represent, for the natural body, several individuals. Therefore, cells represent local members, tissues represent district members, organs or parts represent state members, systems represent regional members, and the entire body represents national members. Unlike the church body, the natural body understands that everything should work interdependently.

Certain cells, tissue, organs, or systems are not thought to be more important or having a more important function than the rest. And the natural body still remains highly organized and structured, even unified.

Within the church body, there is always talk of unity. There is always talk of discipline. The natural body understands its purpose: to glorify its creator and to reproduce itself. The church body, on the other hand, looks highly structured and organized, but mass confusion abounds because it has lost its true purpose: to glorify its creator, God, and to win souls for Christ, that is, to reproduce itself. The church body appears to be active. It has immersed itself in programs and projects. These programs and projects exist on every level of the church body. Starting at level 1, the local members, as you travel upward, each level is supposed to participate in the programs and projects of the level just above them. So we see how much stress and strain this puts on those at the lower levels. This represents the "life blood" being sucked out of the members. Those at the lowest level feel the stress and strain most of all. Because not only are those at the lower levels supposed to participate in the programs and projects of those at all the levels above them, but they are also required to or expected to participate in the programs and projects of those at the same level. This not only represents energy and time being taken away from each member accomplishing its true purpose, but money appears to be the basis of the meeting and participation. Each level is required or supposed to give a "report," that is, a certain amount of money each month, each quarter, or each year, depending on how that particular denomination sets its reporting period. Also, each member on the same level, out of love, wants to help out and support other members in their programs and projects with time and money – the church body's natural resources.

There are some denominations or church groups that will boldly tell their members or congregations during their church or pastoral anniversary that it's "about money." To be fair, most of the churches feel they must do this. Love is no longer the basis for giving. It has become something done out of duty and requirement. This is totally opposite of what Paul advocated. The highly organized form has made it this way. The members feel the drain on their time and pocketbooks, not only from their local churches, but at every district, state, regional, and national meeting. Every member knows that something is wrong, even those at the higher levels can sense it. But they are all caught in a knot that no one seems to have the courage or the wisdom to unravel. In essence, no one wants to admit that "the emperor has on no clothes." When some of those at each level do attempt to unravel the knot or even suggest that there is a knot and it needs unraveling, they are labeled as dissenters, those causing contention, "mavericks," or even "bootleg preachers." Heads of churches have even stated that these types, although called by God to teach or preach His word, would never be utilized by them or sanctioned by them simply because they did not come up from within their denominations or another recognized and acceptable church group.

The church has forgotten its true purpose. It has already experienced at least one heart attack. Doctors tell us that a heart attack is the first sign of heart disease. Most people don't survive this warning. The church is surviving, but it has become weak. The enemy has moved in. Some say that the devil comes to church every time there is a service. This is definitely true. There are several reasons why he feels so welcomed. First of all, some are only pretending, that is, they are, in essence, "false prophets in sheep clothing" (Matt. 7:15). Second, the enemy's goal is to wreak havoc and dissension within the body. But lately, he feels welcome because he is so happy to see the charismatic church members shouting, singing, and praising God – only within their individual four walls. He is happy that this is contained and that not very many of those who are unsaved get to hear the preaching and teaching because frankly most of them aren't within those four walls of the church, and may never attend. Satan is thrilled that the body is doing all of these "good" programs and projects that have absolutely nothing to do with winning souls for Christ. He is thrilled that the members are being zapped of their time, energy, and money, because of the highly structured and organized body. And he is especially pleased that instead of utilizing the moneys to send out or disperse its members to "all the ends of the earth" to "preach the gospel" (Matt. 16:15), that the leaders are building bigger and better church buildings to house more inactive members, that is, those whose love has grown cold along with the leaders, when it comes to winning souls for Christ. And most of all, he is pleased because many Christians are bound by demonic spirits. We always look for the "snake" eyes, foul breath, or violent personality. But spirits come in other subtle forms also. We must beware because the enemy can appear "as an angel of light" (2 Cor. 11:14).

Chapter 4. Dead vs. Living Cells

"The dead do not praise the Lord, nor any
who go down into silence."
(Psalm 115:17)

<u>Dead Cells</u>

The hardest chapter to write is the one you live personally; the one that exposes you for what you really are. However, no matter how much you avoid it you end up "writing" that chapter by the life you live because it shows through. The hope exists because as long as you feel "dead" and realize the need to be revived, means you have not truly died yet.

On a human body, dead cells exist as an outgrowth from that which is living, breathing, thriving, and productive. They are still attached to the body, but no longer serve in the actual growth and re-creation of the body. For example, our hair and nails are dead cells. Nothing can truly "hurt" these cells, which means nothing can truly reach these cells anymore. They have surpassed all vulnerability, and therefore, have surpassed all feeling.

So, too, individuals in church who have ceased being productive in the body of Christ, can be fooled into thinking they are alive when they are really dead. They go through the motions. They sing, they dance and shout, they mouth the words to Scripture, and they can even recite Scripture when need be from rote memory. But their hearts are hard and calloused. Their spirits are void of life and vigor. They have grieved the Holy Spirit over and over again by their disobedience to God, and now the Holy Spirit no longer abides. They can no longer praise God the way they once did. They are caught up in a web that sin has woven.

Not only can individual members exist in the body as dead cells, but so too can those who are supposed to be in leadership over us and supposed to serve as our examples. "To him much is given, much is required" (Luke 12:48). These words burn like bullets within the souls of leaders, constantly convicted of the responsibility that rests upon their shoulders. Paul said, "I keep under my body and bring it under subjection, lest I preach to you and I myself become a castaway" (1 Cor. 9:27).

We see leaders today who will just get out of the bed of adultery and go straight into the pulpit and "preach the house down." God says his gifts and callings are without repentance. He gives his leaders charisma, intellect, and influence. These traits are supposed to draw multitudes to Christ so that the Lord can remake them, remold them, and present them blameless before the Holy Father. But many leaders have allowed the enemy to darken their souls and their intentions. They have become tainted with the stain of lust of the eyes and flesh. Instead of drawing multitudes to Christ, they draw multitudes to themselves. You then have a case of the "blind leading the blind." With such, God is not pleased. God's displeasure leads to God's chastisement. Since everything belongs to Him, it is also in His power to take it all away. God removed the anointing from King Saul. However, Saul, now dead, continued to operate as if he was still the Lord's anointed. Yet, in reality, Saul was a completely dead cell in the body of Christ.

Living Cells

It is not hard to see the difference between dead cells and those that are alive. In fact, we can tell the difference in everything in our lives and in the world around us. We see the difference between a green leaf and a dried twig. We see the difference between a beautiful serene, blue, lake of flowing, reviving, life-giving water, and that of a dry, dusty, and dirt-filled ravine with dead men's bones. We see the difference between a human body that is alive, healthy, dynamic, moving, and active – and that of one which has ceased to move, ceased to breathe life-giving air, without sight and hearing, and stiff because Rigor Mortis has set in due to the cessation of blood flow to vital parts of the body.

What has caused this? The answer is simply – sin. Sin, when it has conceived, brings forth death, as the Scripture says. Sin brings in hardness of soul, stiffness of mind, and dryness of morals. But sin is not satisfied with its status as sin. The enemy longs to have it not only infiltrate every fabric of society and the church, yet longs and works exceedingly hard to have sin accepted and acknowledged as "true," "good," "honorable," "respected," and "right." If Satan can gain this victory, he feels he has won the controversy with God and feels he has beaten God, even though Satan lost the victory a long time ago. However, he longs to have others deceived (dead) like he is.

The Bible depicts a reprobate mind as someone who, despite the evidence and statements in the Bible to the contrary, chooses to believe, based on popular belief that what he is doing is right, and lives a life of sin. The Bible says that "there is a way that seems right to a man but the end thereof is death (Prov. 14:12). We are sinful, human beings.

All have sinned and come short of the glory of God. In this natural state, our ways are not God's ways. This means that the non-regenerated mind and heart is in no condition and shape to contemplate and understand spiritual things. One thing that people forget is that Christ did not save us "in our sins," but He saved us "from our sins." For a person to become a Christian, that person has to first believe in his or her heart that Christ is the Son of God who was crucified and rose from the dead, and that He sits on the right hand of the Father making intercession for us. Now, when a person accepts Christ, that person is a follower of Christ and believes what Christ believes. That person agrees, as Christ does, that sin is wrong, that all unrighteousness is sin, that there is no big or little sin. That person now believes and agrees with the Word of God, which is the Bible. This should be the person's standard, not what the person sees on T.V., not what the person hears others say, not what the government says is right and wrong. It is a known fact that the government's laws, that is, things that are legal, do not always line up with the Word of God. The lawmakers do not use the Word of God as their standard when enacting or passing laws. The law says that abortion is legal because it defines "life" differently than how God defines "life." The Bible says that "before you were formed in your mother's womb, I knew you." Therefore, God creates life and man is procreator.

We must judge our actions and beliefs on what God says and not man. Case in point: homosexuality. Man says homosexuality is right and it's good. The Bible says that is sin and is wrong. According to the Word of God, there is no such thing as a Christian homosexual. These two things are in opposition to each other. Anyone who says and does contrary to God's word is deceived. That is, that person is a dead cell. This is part of Satan's infiltration into the church. Only God's true believers will continue to seek God and be faithful to His Word. Satan uses sex sins because sex is so powerful that it creates life. Just this one fact: that sex was intended to create life, shows that God has no use for homosexuality and does not approve of it. Also, it should be noted that being a kind and good person is not a requirement for being a Christian. It is good to be a good and kind person, but the Bible says no one is good from God's point of view. We must be born again. We must be reconciled back to God because of Adam's sin. One thing people must realize is if it is okay to do any and every thing we think we want to do, and still say we are Christians, there would have been no need for Christ to die, that is, to pay for our sins. This is because, as Satan has been attempting to make a case, if there is no sin, then there is no need for a savior, and man is therefore his own god, and finally, has no need of God. This is total and complete death of a once-living and breathing cell.

How to Live and Not Die (Spiritually)

The Spirit makes intercession for us; the Spirit brings all things back to our remembrance; the Spirit searches the deep things of God, and the Spirit leads us into all truth. It is easy to tell which churches do not have God's Spirit. Your spirit will bear witness that it's missing – and it will usually have the tell-tale sign of the stench of sin. This does not mean that it is full of members who never sin; it means that sin permeates the place, from the head of the church on down, and stinks to high heaven.

The Holy Ghost is God's S.O.S. pad. It "Scrubs Out Sin," and keeps it out on a daily basis. The church that uses the cleaning agent is able to rightly divide the Word of God. They work hand in hand to cleanse the spiritual bodies of its members, so that all will come out smelling clean, fresh, and renewed.

Dressed To Kill

Once the bodies are clean, they are ready to get dressed. We dress our natural bodies daily, searching through our filled-to-the-rim closets to find the right outfit for the right occasion. We automatically know what outfit is appropriate for what occasion. We discern between a formal affair and an informal affair. We discern between the proper dress for work and the proper dress for play. We even know what colors go well with what occasion.

For the spiritual body, there is one and only one outfit here on earth that God provided: His Whole Armor. Each day we are to wear this spiritual clothing. One size fits all. However, the Armor does not adjust itself to fit the contours of the body, but rather the body adjusts itself to fit the contours of the Armor. The Armor never changes and never wears out. Some have tried to adjust the Armor, and found themselves instead naked and without protective clothing. Each part of the Armor serves a specifically defined purpose.

The Belt of Truth

This belt is Jesus Christ who said "I am the way, the truth, and the life. No man cometh to the Father except by me" (John 14:6). This belt holds up every other item of clothing. Without it, everything else would soon fall down, leaving the body naked and vulnerable. This belt has many holes, representing the holes Christ received from the crown on thorns placed on His head, the open wounds from the whip, the spear piercing His side, and the nails in His hands and feet. Newly-born Christians have to use the last hole of the belt because initially the belt is much too big for them. As they grow, they can measure their growth because they move up to the next hole, and to the next. They are growing into the fullness of Christ. God is changing them from "glory to glory" (Isaiah 28:10). There are those who have tried to change the Belt of Truth into a lie. They say that the story of Christ is a man-made story or that Jesus did live, but He was only a good man, a prophet perhaps, but surely not the Son of God. Some believe that we are all gods and that Jesus is not the one and only way to God. But the Bible says that "he who does not have the son does not have life" (1 John 5:12). Either you believe the word of God or you don't. There is no middle ground. Jesus said if you're not for me you are against me. Therein is the spirit of the anti-Christ. They are against God's true teachings. They are against God's laws and His ways of doing things. They are against God's righteousness and believe they can live any way they please. They are of the "Burger King" generation who shout "give us the love and prosperity but hold the justice." We can't have it our way; it has to be God's way. His way is the only way for true peace, joy, and eternal life. There are those who will follow the "Burger King" churches because "The Belt of Lies" fits them a whole lot better and they are to wear it on the first hole immediately. There is no waiting period of growth, because no growth is needed. Everything goes. However, this piece of the garment will not hold up the rest of the pieces of the garment, causing the entire attire to retire to the ground. These will find themselves naked when Christ returns. And just as Christ said in the parable to those who were found without the proper garments at the wedding feast, they will be cast out, symbolizing their banishment from the presence of God into the pit of Hell.

The Breastplate of Righteousness

This Breastplate is Christ's righteousness, not ours. It is there to protect our most valuable parts, such as our heart, our stomach, our kidneys, and our spleen. The Bible says "keep your heart with all diligence, for out of it are the issues of life" (Prov. 4:23). It is easy to see how one piece of the Armor builds on the other. Without the Belt of Truth, that is belief and faith in Christ, you cannot take upon His righteousness. This is because an non-regenerated heart has not repented, and therefore cannot receive Christ's justification, and cannot receive propitiation for sins, and consequently, cannot and do not have the right to Christ's glorification.

The Shield of Faith

This Shield is to protect the body against the fiery darts and spears of the Evil One. It is used to deflect those attacks. These attacks will come against all who will live godly in Christ Jesus (2 Tim. 3:12). It will not depend on a feeling or emotion, but your assurance that you have taken on Christ's righteousness. By faith, you believe, and so by faith, you wield your shield wherever it is needed. It is there to protect all the parts of the body. It is not stationary like the other parts, but can move wherever and as fast as needed.

The Helmet of Salvation

Upon the head of every member of the church body should sit the Helmet of Salvation. This is to protect our minds from the Devil's lies. We have been assured that Christ has died and has paid the penalty for all of our sins once we repent, and that we are truly saved from the Lake of Fire, reserved for Satan and his angels (Rev. 20:10). This item on the head is God's protective covering to protect our minds from evil thoughts and from doubt. The Bible tells us that "whatsoever things are true, whatsoever things are pure, whatsoever things are lovely, if there be any virtue, any praise, any good report, think on these things" (Phil. 4:8). This is the substance of what faith is made. They are the strong support the mind needs to hold up under the Devil's evil attacks. The Bible says that "whatsoever a man thinks in his heart so is he" (Prov. 23:7). If we think on the good and claim God's promises we are protecting ourselves. Satan can try to bump, thump, ping, ding, bombard, dynamite, even nuclear bomb us with whatever he chooses, but nothing the Devil has can penetrate God's mighty "force-field." The Bible says God is our rock, our fortress, our shield, and our high tower. It says, in Psalm 91, that we can abide in the "shadow of the Almighty," for the Lord God is "my refuge and my fortress: my God; in him will I trust." (Psalm 91:2). God promises to "give his angels charge over thee, to keep thee in all thy ways," and to finally, the Lord says that "with long life will I satisfy him [us], and show him [us] my salvation." (Psalm 91:11, 16)

The Gospel of Peace

This piece of the Armor we wear on our feet. We stand on our feet. We walk and run on our feet. Every part of the foot connects to and is sensitive to all the parts of the body. When our feet hurt, our whole body hurts. God gives us two for balance. This is to balance our dual nature: we are human, natural beings of flesh, but we are also spiritual beings of God's spirit dwelling within us, constantly regenerating us. Wherever we travel, wherever God leads His people, the church should be ready and prepared to deliver the Good News, that is, the message of salvation to all who will receive it. This message should be carried in love and in peace. The church body should be as humble, meek, and non-threatening as possible. However, this does not mean that the church should be weak and compromising. Meekness and weakness are not the same. Meekness can be defined as "harnessed strength." God tells us to be "harmless as doves and wise as serpents" (Matt. 10:16). The church should be unwavering and uncompromising with sin. The heart of the church should go out to the sinner, welcoming the one who is wayward into the fold, or in the case of the backslider, welcoming this one back into the fold. However, the Bible also says that if they will not receive you, "shake off the dust from your feet," and move on (Matt. 10:14).

The Sword of The Spirit

This last, but not least, all important piece completes the Armor – without it, the church is incomplete and does not bear the "Whole Armor." Jesus said he came to bring a "sword," that is, a spiritual sword. We are in a spiritual battle, not a physical one. The Word of God is "quick and powerful, sharper than one two-edged sword, piercing even to the dividing asunder of joint and marrow, soul and spirit, and is a discerner of the thoughts and intents of the heart" (Heb. 4:12). This is the only weapon of offense that God gives with the Armor. All of the other pieces of the Armor are weapons of defense. The Word of God is Jesus as He is revealed in scripture. Before one can truly know and understand who Jesus is, one must be convicted by the Holy Spirit. And it is God who is sending the message. These three agree as one. This Word of God is not just to be carried around physically, but God says to write His word upon our hearts (Heb. 8:10). This Sword of the Spirit will not only light our paths, but will blind our enemies so that they are humbled and subdued (1 Chr. 17:10). Whatever foul devices the demons had planned for us, they will surely fall prey to themselves in their own traps (Esther 7:10). An example is Saul's experience on his way to Damascus, in which he met the Lord Jesus Christ and no longer persecuted the church, but became its biggest advocate and defender (Acts 9:1-7).

There are so many faithful ones: Abraham, Isaac, Joseph, Moses, Joshua, Esther, Elijah, Jeremiah, the Apostles, including Paul, John the Revelator, and of course, Christ, just to name only a few – those living, breathing, dynamic cells of the spiritual body, the church. Many suffered persecution and died a martyr's death, but they "finished the race," they "finished the course" that was set before them, and they pressed toward the "prize of the high calling in Christ" (Phil. 3:14). They counted everything they gave up for the "excellency of Christ" as "dung," and instead, reaching

forward for the crown of salvation (Phil. 3:8). Further reading

and studying of their lives can teach us how to live and not

die.

Chapter 5. Out of Sight, Out of Mind

*"Do not enter into judgment with your servant, for in your sight
no one living is righteous."
(Psalm 143:2)*

The natural body is composed of many internal parts –
those parts which are necessary and vital, but those which we
cannot see with the human eye. In fact, some of them we refer
to as "unmentionable" parts (1 Cor. 12:23). They are
considered of lesser value even though we could not live
without them. They have been exploited by the pornographic
industry and made to appear as something ugly and
disgusting – so much so, that people detest the parts that God
provided for the body. They are degraded and used to satisfy
the sick lusts of voyeurs. Millions of dollars are made on them
each year.

But God said everything He created was good (Genesis
1:31). Every part of the natural body has usefulness and has a
purpose no matter where it is located and no matter what
other's popular opinion of that particular part. It is still vital

and necessary for life. The same is true of the spiritual body's deeply hidden parts. Used for the proper purpose and in the right manner, these members will produce other church bodies. Churches love to talk about unity and quote scriptures that refer to unity, such as Psalm 133. However, most of them only think the scripture refers to their own specific denomination, or even worse, they believe it refers only to their local church. But everyone who is called by the name of Christ is considered a part of the "brethren" (1 Peter 3:8). It is true that God did not make denominations – man did. But God gave the churches different personalities, different strengths, different gifts, and different ways of working and using these gifts – all toward the same purpose: to point the lost to Christ. When God says to speak the same things and be of the same mind, He did not mean that everybody should believe exactly the same way on matters that are not specifically stated in scripture. God means that there should be a unity of purpose and goal in sharing the Good News of salvation through repentance and acceptance of Jesus Christ as one's personal savior.

For natural bodies to unite and procreate, there must be male and female, that is, there must be two separate bodies, essentially the same in the important parts, and different only in shape, form, and function of one of the reproductive parts. It is this union that will produce another life form to carry forth when the two parent bodies have accomplished their separate and combined purposes and have lived out their life terms. This is the same with the church body. There is often no unity because many cannot accept the fact that at least one part of the body is not supposed to be exactly, that is, identical in shape, form, and function as another part of the body. It all fits together perfectly and is perfectly joined in unity when applied appropriately.

This is why women's so-called liberation movement and homosexuality was and is a useful tool for the devil. The enemy knew that if it was carried out to the extreme that a wedge would be driven even further to separate men and women. He knew that homosexuality would take an even stronger foothold and abound significantly to combat God's true plan for creation. If this were to continue, man would eventually annihilate himself. Sex is a powerful force, so powerful that it creates life. For everything God has that is good, the Devil devises a counterfeit to counteract God's plans. But as always, God will have the last say, rendering the Devil's devices of none effect.

If the spiritual body, the church, keeps fighting against each other and competing with each other, as do the sexes at times, instead of combining their efforts, the church, as Jesus intended, would also become extinct. However, since Jesus told Peter that "upon this rock I will build my church [the power of the Holy Ghost] and the gates of Hell shall not prevail against it" (Matt. 16:18), we know and understand that Jesus will return for His bride, the church, before it can totally be destroyed by the enemy. Unfortunately, only a remnant (certain parts) will be saved, not the entire body. Many who believe since they are part of the head, hands, eyes, or what is believed to be the more "important parts," may have a rude awakening to learn that the hidden and seemingly insignificant and less comely parts will be in that remnant instead. To some, Christ will say, "I never knew you" (Matt. 7:23).

The Deformed Body

One denominational church in which I was a member had a visiting female pastor/prophetess/teacher. Her manner of working and operating in her spiritual gifts was a lot different than what many of the people in the congregation expected. She prophesied both natural and spiritual blessings to the people and she also gave words of knowledge as the Spirit led her. Many times we hear prophecies and then sit back, waiting for it to drop out of the sky like the manna from heaven that the Israelites received in the wilderness. This is why many of us miss our blessing and all that God has in store for us. God does and can work miracles, but he will not perform miracles just for the sake of performing a miracle. When He can accomplish his purposes through natural means, He will. For example, God does not need us to help him in bringing people to accept Christ as their Savior. But in His infinite wisdom, love, and graciousness, He allows us the privilege to participate in His great plan.

As far as receiving His blessings, our lives must line up with His perfect will. And, we must believe and accept what God has promised to us. One of the members at the church was in a wheelchair. Her body was deformed. The Lord showed me that her body represented not only that particular denominational church's body, but all churches like them. The prophetess did some deliberate and explicit things. Those who were not tuned into her may have missed the significance. The prophetess gracefully and delicately removed the leg supports from the girl's weak feet. She then pressed the girl's feet to her body so that her legs were outstretched. The prophetess then began to anoint the entire length of the girl's legs and feet. In other words, she was giving extra attention to those members of the body that had been neglected for so long a time. She then prayed powerful words of healing to the girl. She then had someone help her to remove the girl from the wheelchair so that she could go forth in the healing she had received. The girl walked, but with a twisted foot, and deformity of the right side. Finally, she went back to her wheelchair.

The Lord showed me that the girl had been healed; however, her mind had not believed, nor received that healing. This represented the church body. When the head is sick, the whole body is sick. The head, because of disbelief, no longer looks up to God but rather the head starts to look downward. It becomes confused. Its vision is dimmed. Its hearing is dulled. And it starts to speak inappropriately, all of this because it is now sending the wrong messages and signals to the parts of the body, including that which controls speech. It no longer looks outwardly, that is, to go forth and do what God has ordained it to do. Instead, everything is turned inwardly on itself. For example, church going has become an end in and of itself, rather than with the purpose of "refueling" itself to witness to a dying world so that all might be saved. It feeds only its own needs, not the needs of the community. And since the head is confused, it focuses mainly on certain parts of its body. In fact, it favors other members of the body over others. This is what causes its deformity, especially when it tries to walk. The neglected members are inactive, sluggish, and unproductive from lack of use. The head may even rebuke and chastise those parts for being inactive and unproductive, not realizing that the head is the reason for those members being in such a state.

So what happens to the head when it sees other bodies that are healthy, strong, moving, and walking upright, straight and tall? It feels uncomfortable. So it searches around for that comfort zone – that wheelchair. The wheelchair is the man-made traditions of the church's denomination. The crutch that the head can rely on to give it an excuse for binding itself and its members in place – an excuse for not going forward – an excuse for not changing – and a way to keep everything status quo and under control. Only the head and leadership (the shoulders and parts of the upper torso) can move around. They are still bound, but not as much as the rest of the body.

Chapter 6. Feeding the Body

"I will feed them in good pasture, and their fold shall be on the high mountains of Israel."
(Ezekiel 34:14)

Without the proper nutrition, the physical body would be sorely malnourished, resulting in a degenerative mind, polluted blood, nervous irritability, and a breakdown in the body's in-born immunity system – allowing no protection from bacteria and disease. The body would eventually wither and die.

Just as the proper diet of good wholesome stimulant-free foods are essential to good health, so too is the "Bread of Life" important for spiritual development. "Jesus said unto them, verily, verily, I say unto you, except ye eat the flesh of the Son of man, and drink his blood, ye have no life in you" (John 6:53). And just as it is important for the physical body to abstain from unhealthy food and stimulants, so too the spiritual body, while relying on nourishment from the Word of God, must abstain from partaking only of misleading and self-destructing worldly entertainment, that is geared toward only exciting the senses but does nothing to teach, enlighten, or uplift the mental or spiritual faculties. There should be a healthy balance.

Food is not eaten merely to gratify hunger pains, but mainly to receive the essential nutrients into the blood stream to produce a healthy and highly effective body. So, too, the Word of God is read not only for the sake of knowledge, but to increase faith. "Faith comes by hearing and hearing by the Word of God" (Romans 10:17). It is needed to grow toward sanctification. "Desire the sincere milk of the word that you may grow thereby" (1 Peter 2:2). And, it is needed as protection against the wiles of the enemy – that is, it is the "sword of the Spirit" (Ephesians 6:17). It is only when we are weak and malnourished that the body is defenseless against all manners of illnesses and disease. So, too, spiritual vitality relies on nourishment of pure Scripture in the form of daily devotional reading, careful and prayerful study, Bible lesson study, and extensive scriptural reading. All of this will not only give Bible knowledge, but bring the body into a communicative relationship with God – whereby He will reveal His character and nature, His promises, His expectations, His will, His Kingdom, and His Son who is the embodiment and flesh of God's Word. So let us eat, lest we starve.

Proper Digestion

Food, no matter how nourishing, is useless until it is properly digested and utilized. Before food can be used effectively by the body to make good blood the food must be broken down bit by bit. The digestive system ensures that all parts of the body receive the proper nutrients. In other words, the food is applied to the body and in effect, converts the body into an active, thriving, and usable and worthwhile system. The body, thus having applied the necessary nutrients to its parts and throughout its system, is ready to dispel the impurities that have accumulated within its system. The same is true for the spiritual body, the church. The word of God though read and studied for an endless amount of time, will avail nothing if not utilized and applied to our lives, that is, lived out in the body itself. The apostle James says "but be ye doers of the word, and not hearers only, deceiving your own selves" (James 1:22). Each member must digest the word, slowly, carefully, and prayerfully. The Holy Spirit, the Divine Teacher, breaks down the word of God into "bite size" chews, allowing the word to be slowly savored (meditation), swallowed (obeyed), and converted through the digestive process to make good blood. As the apostle Paul stated: "The word of God is quick, and powerful, piercing even to the dividing asunder of soul and spirit, and of the joints and marrow, and is a discerner of the thoughts and intents of the heart" (Hebrews 4:12). This leads to a pure and holy life committed entirely to Christ.

Amino Acids, Vitamins, and Minerals

If a body is to maintain good health, it must have a steady and proper supply of vitamins and minerals, usually found in herbal combinations or in foods. Amino acids are the nucleus of every living cell. They are the basis of life itself. In their proper balance, they serve as a great power in restoring and maintaining good health. We call them "essential amino acids" and "non-essential amino acids." However, all of them are necessary to the building up of the body. Most of the 22 identifiable amino acids can be manufactured by the body, but eight of them cannot and must be supplied by the diet. That is, the food nutrition must supply them. For the spiritual body, the amino acids' nucleus is the word made flesh, that is, Jesus Christ. The Bible says that "all things were created by him and there was nothing made that was not made by him." He is the nucleus, or at the center and heart of the church body. Within each cell of each member is that quickening, living, breathing, regenerating faith through grace. Just as the natural body is depleted of the necessary nutrients as it exerts energy each day, it must put back these necessary nutrients to maintain an active, healthy body. For example, Leucine is an amino acid. It is necessary for growth, stimulates the brain functions, is essential for blood development, regulates the digestion and metabolism, assists the functions of the glandular system and increases the muscular energy levels. Lysine is essential to ensure adequate absorption of calcium and formation of collagen necessary to bone, cartilage and connective tissue. But before lysine can be utilized in the formation of collagen, it needs Vitamin C. Without Vitamin C or adequate protein to supply the amino acid lysine, the body would not heal properly and would be more susceptible to infection. As we can see, there is an interrelationship of the various nutrients. Lysine also strengthens the circulatory system and maintains normal growth of cells. It also controls acid, alkaline balance, building blocks of blood antibodies, may lessen incidence of certain kinds of cancer, and regulates the pineal and mammary glands and functions of the gall bladder. We see that amino acids are necessary to the life of the cell, especially lysine. Although amazing that one amino acid would be responsible for so much; however, like certain parts of the spiritual body, we know that "to him much is given, much is required" (Luke 12:48)

Vitamins and minerals are what make the body strong and healthy. When certain ones are lacking, the body suffers. For example, vitamin A is an infection fighter, which builds bones and teeth, prolongs longevity and delays senility, and maintains and repairs healthy tissue. Another example is when the body is lacking in iron. Iron is the anti-anemia mineral and to be absorbed effectively into the body, Calcium and Copper must be present. Iron also combines with protein to form hemoglobin, improves protein metabolism, and is needed to bring oxygen to the lungs and to the body's muscular cells. Iron improves circulation, intensifies mental vitality, and is important for the liver, kidney, and heart. It is also needed in digestion and elimination, and it, along with oxygen, promotes youthfulness. Without the necessary vitamins and minerals, the body's immune system will gradually break down, and consequently, it will die.

Although all the amino acids, vitamins, and minerals, whether acquired in food sources of herb, are necessary for the body, we will liken the 10 B-vitamins to the spiritual gifts. Just as these vitamins are necessary for the building up the body, so too, spiritual gifts, properly administered and allowed to flow freely throughout the body, will "perfect the saints," will allow the body to work and minister, and will "edify" or build up the body. The body can work and minister because each member is perfected or made whole because each cell, tissue, and part is built up and nourished. And that nourishment comes from "speaking the truth in love" so that we may "grow up into him in all things, which is the head, even Christ; from whom the whole body fitly joined together and compacted by that which every joint supplieth, according to the effectual working in the measure of every part, maketh increase of the body unto the edifying of itself in love" (Ephesians 4:15-16)

Vitamin B1 – Pastoring

Vitamin B1 (Thiamine) is called the "morale" vitamin. It is essential for the health of the entire nervous system, and serves 12 functions. So, too, the pastor is responsible for the health of the entire church body and the bishop for the entire organization of church bodies. They too serve many functions.

The proper functioning of the digestive system – Vitamin B1 makes sure that the complete digestive system is in proper working order. The pastor or bishop makes sure that the congregation does everything in order and functions smoothly. The pastor must make sure that the word is properly "divided" or broken down so that the congregation is able to receive the word and properly digest it.

Aiding the growth of young children – Vitamin B1 is especially needed to make sure that young children grow properly. The pastor makes sure that babies and young saints are growing with ease and without discouragement to the point that they are stifled, immobilized, or become stagnant. The pastor knows that without growth, the baby or young saint will die.

Assisting the body to utilize energy from carbohydrate foods – Vitamin B1 helps the body take the energy applied from carbohydrates and use it. If the calories are not used, the body can become obese and lazy. The pastor encourages the congregation to use the knowledge and zeal it acquires by exercising its faith in the form of witnessing, evangelism, street ministry, giving of selves, and also to work within the church by serving.

Needed during pregnancy, lactation, and during strenuous exercise – These are periods of extra stress and heaviness on the body. Just as Vitamin B1 is needed because it helps the body during these heavy times, so too, the pastor helps the congregation during the time of "pregnancy," that is, a time when the church is about to experience a "birth" of a ministry that will spring from its loins. The pastor will even have to be there for support and encouragement to make sure the "baby" receives its nourishment and nurturing.

Nourishing the brain, eyes, ears, hair, heart, liver, and kidneys – Vitamin B1 supplies nourishment to the main and central parts of the body that are responsible for communicating – sending, decoding, receiving, and expelling fluids throughout the body. The pastor supplies nourishment to the main and central parts of the body that are responsible for sending, decoding, receiving, and expelling vital information throughout the church body. He may even at times give special attention to these areas because their effectiveness may depend on the pastor's nourishment.

Building the blood – Vitamin B1 fortifies and builds up the cells within the blood. Since the blood is the life of the body, this function is so essential. The pastor works at building the life-blood within the congregation. He knows that without this good blood, the body will die.

Maintaining the intestines and stomach – Vitamin B1 maintains the intestinal and stomach wall to prevent indigestion. The pastor maintains the walls of the intestinal and stomach area of the congregation. Through gentleness, love, and patience, he helps clear away debris and bacteria to make sure there is a smooth reception area for the word of God so that is can be properly digested. He or she governs the way the word is administered so that raw foods, which digest first, are served first, and cooked foods, which take longer to digest, are served next, and desserts, which are served last, are kept to a minimum so as not to overpower the healthy meal.

Alleviating pain – Vitamin B1 eases the pain within the body that causes irritability. The pastor comforts the body. He or she tries to relieve the anguish, mental stress, and ease the trials the body experiences through counseling, understanding, and prayer.

<u>Preventing excess fatty deposits on wall of arteries</u> – Vitamin B1 prevents excessive fatty deposits that can clog up the walls of the arteries and lead to congestive heart failure. The pastor takes steps to make sure that there is a smooth and even flow of blood throughout the body by making sure that "fat deposits" due to too much sugar in the diet don't clog up and stifle the heart of the word.

<u>Repelling the bite of insects</u> – Vitamin B1 serves as a repellent against the bite of insects. It helps prevent the poison from entering into the bloodstream and prevents the infection of the skin. The pastor helps repel the biting effects of jealousy and envy that creeps up and infiltrates the congregation. He or she knows this is a device from the enemy, and the pastor wisely prevents this poison from entering the bloodstream of the congregation by making sure

that every member is treated with respect, with love, and allowed to go forth in the gift and calling given them by God.

Protecting against the effects of lead (poisoning) – Vitamin B1 protects against the effects of the heavy weight placed on the body due to lead entering the body. The pastor protects against the effects of the heavy weight of the storms, the trials, and tribulations of the congregation's lives, whether due to sin or disobedience, causing them to be out of the will of God. As a follower of Christ means that we will always encounter trials and tribulations. However, the pastor can, through correction, rebuke, chastening, and encouragement (all by the word of God) make sure the heavy weight does not affect and spread to the entire body.

Vitamin B2 – Giving

This vitamin is called the "youth vitamin." It is essential for proper enzyme formation, normal growth, formation of tissue, metabolism of fats, carbohydrates and protein. It also helps maintain good vision, skin, nails, and hair. It is essential for antibody formation, sodium, potassium balance, production of red blood cells and hormones, absorption of iron, helps provide extra stamina and is essential during periods of lactation. Just as an enzyme functions as a biochemical catalyst for the human body, so too giving within the body produces a healthy cycle within the spiritual body to keep it youthful and moving. The Bible says "give and it shall be given to you, pressed down, shaken together, and running over, shall men give unto your bosom; for with the same measure that you mete withal, it shall be measure to you again." This kind of giving, sacrificial as Jesus did, without being contentious, is what guards against needless decay because it is constantly shedding off the old and putting on the new. The giver is giving of its time, money, effort, and self-preparing itself to receive. In this way, it helps keep the body well balanced.

Vitamin B3 – Preaching

This vitamin assists the body to perform energy producing reactions in cells. It converts amino acid tryptophan into niacin, promotes good physical and mental health, aids in healthy skin, tongue and digestive system, regulates levels of blood, preventing high cholesterol and high blood pressure and heart attacks. So too, sound and pure preaching of the word of God performs energy producing repentant reactions in sinners. The power of the Holy Spirit convicts hearts and converts them to the truth. Sound and undiluted preaching, that is, the spreading and proclaiming of the gospel, administered and interpreted by the Holy Ghost who alone knows the hearts of man, controls or regulates the intensity of the impact of the Word on each individual heart.

Vitamin B9 – Teaching

This vitamin is essential for the entire nervous system to stimulate production of hydrochloric acid formation of genetic cells: DNA and RNA. It is also essential for the absorption of iron and calcium with vitamin B12 and Vitamin C to break down protein foods, for the formation of new red blood cells, for the production of antibodies, and for the maintenance of sex organs. Just as sound preaching is needed, sound and pure teaching is needed even more so. While preaching may convert the sinner, teaching will stimulate growth not only of the newly saved individual, but that individual will teach what they have been taught. Like fruit will produce like fruit. Just as a father's DNA will make his son's DNA, so too the saved individual who is taught sound teaching will produce others by his sound teaching. Teaching helps take the word of God, and by example, illustration, parable, and application of the word, breaks it down into small enough units to be absorbed by the body. Sound teaching can also produce antibodies to protect the body from false teaching and from infections due to sin. Teaching will maintain the body's reproductive function. Good teaching will equip the body with wisdom to choose the good, the holy, the pure, the righteous, and to reject that which is contrary to holiness, purity, and righteousness.

Vitamin B17 – Prophesying

This is said to be a very controversial vitamin. It is only legal in 15 states. It contains natural cyanide used to kill cancer cells. It was rejected by the FDA due to its cyanide content because they felt it might be poisonous. On the other hand, it is believed by others to have cancer-controlling and preventive properties that literally poison the malignant cells while nourishing all the other cells. It also stimulates the hemoglobin or red cell count. In the same way, prophesying is very controversial in the church body. It is only accepted and recognized as a legitimate gift of the Spirit in some of the churches. Prophesying is used to kill the cancerous cells of the church body. Usually these cancerous cells are identified by the prophet of God as spiritual apathy, idolatry, blatant sin, religious pride, religious spirit due to traditions that make the "word of God of none effect" (Mark 7:13), and hypocrisy.

Sometimes prophecy is rejected, even by higher religious authorities, because they feel it might be damaging to the body. Even though the prophet is led of God (or should be), the leaders will usually caution the prophet to be very careful and consider what he or she says, how he or she says it, to whom, and when and where he or she says it. The leader always considers the impact the prophecy will have on their flock, as well they should. However, like vitamin B17, prophesying, when done by the Holy Spirit's leading and control, has "disease" controlling and preventive properties which call out, convict, tear down, and destroy "malignant and diseased" cells, while at the same time nourishing the good cells. This works on the same principle that John talks about: "in him (Jesus) was life, and the life was the light of men. And the light shines in darkness, and the darkness comprehended it not" (John 1:4-5). Because the people reject this light (Jesus) and God's many messengers (prophets), just like the Pharisees and Sadducees of Jesus' day, the church's immune system slowly breaks down, causing the church to be in danger of contracting A.I.D.S. (Acquired Immunodeficiency Syndrome). Like the physical disease, the white blood cells (converted and dedicated Christians) are slowly being destroyed and rendered ineffective, and the antibodies (Word of God, prayer, fasting, witnessing), have gone neglected, rendering the body helpless against infectious attacks. The culprit: spiritual apathy. The body only cares about filling its "storehouse" to build bigger buildings, which lose so many members each year. The body cares only about appearing righteous and holy on the outside, that is, wearing the right clothes, church etiquette (putting up your finger to go to the bathroom) – all the little traditional things that make them feel they are doing the will of God. Never mind that there is no real love in their hearts. Never mind that souls are dying each day for want of hearing that there is hope in Jesus and salvation for eternal life. Never mind that young people are dropping dead left and right – some whose hearts are failing them – others committing suicide.

Antibody: The Silent Killer

Apathy (antibody) is the lack of interest or concern and is synonymous with "indifference." Webster's New Collegiate Dictionary defines indifference as "the state of being neither excessive nor defective, being neither good nor bad, being neither right nor wrong." However, Jesus put it a better way when He said to the church in Laodicea, through his servant John, "you are neither hot nor cold" (Revelation 5:15 TLB). The Bible foretold of this state of "being lukewarm" or spiritual apathy, but little did we realize that we, who have the truth, would be in that state also. Just as the human body, existing in a state of indifference, neutrality, being impassive, or apathetic, is reduced to a vegetable state – eventually reduced to waiting for the cessation of life, just going through the motions – unaware even when the vital life forces terminate, so too, the spiritual body (church) cannot effectively exist in a state of apathy and indifference. For if there is no consciousness, there is no life. "For the living know that they shall die but the dead know nothing."

(Ecclesiastes 9:5 TLB)

Chapter 7. You Are What You Eat

*"... holding fast to the Head, from whom all the body,
nourished and knit together by joints and ligaments, grows
with the increase that is from God." (Col. 2:19b)*

Food, no matter how nourishing, is useless until is properly digested and utilized. Before the food can be used effectively by the body toward making good blood, it must be broken down into bite-size bits. The digestive system ensures that all parts of the body receive the proper nutrients. In other words, the food is applied to the body and in effect, converts the body into an active, thriving, usable, and worthwhile system. The body, thus having applied the necessary nutrients to its parts and throughout its system, is ready to dispel the impurities which have accumulated within. The same is true for the spiritual body. The word of God, though read and studied for an endless amount of time, will avail nothing if not utilized and applied, that is, it must be lived out in the body. Each member must digest the Word slowly, carefully, and prayerfully. The Holy Spirit breaks down the word of God for easy digestion. However, not everything we hear should be accepted, just like not everything we eat should be or will be digested. For example, if the body consumes spoiled meat, a disease called salmonella can result. This introduces bacteria into the body, causing vomiting and diarrhea. The healthy, intelligent, and knowledgeable body recognizes when something is not healthy, pure, and nutritious food, and consequently, rejects it. So too, the church body should learn not to accept just any kind of teaching, preaching, prophesy, or even miracles. Peter warned against false teachers and false prophets. John warned against the same and also warned that in the last days Satan would come with "all lying wonders and miracles" (2 Thess. 2:9)

Right and sound teaching comes with being able to rightly divide the Word of God. Teachers must study to show themselves approved. Teaching and preaching are all together, though different. A person who preaches is a herald and announces; he or she warns, exhorts, or encourages and quotes scripture (through the Holy Spirit) to make a point. On the other hand, a person who teaches will break down the scripture to make it easy to understand. When studying the Bible it is essential to consider who is speaking, to whom the person is speaking, what issue is involved, the historical time period, and the cultural era, that is, what the customs and traditions were at the time. The Bible is its own interpreter. One must seek out other scriptures to further emphasize what is being taught or learned.

Chapter 8. On The Move

*"Let heaven and earth praise Him, the seas and everything that
moves in them."*
(Psalm 69:34)

Medical reports show that without proper exercise for two weeks, the physical body loses up to 30% of its strength and vitality. Therefore, it would stand to reason that over a significant period of time, lack of exercise (inactivity) would result in complete immobility. The same is true for the exercising of the spiritual body. The use of the limbs of every part of the body is important in good health. For instance, if the feet hurt, the whole body suffers. Every part must be in proper working order to ensure continued healthful life for the entire body. Such is also true for the spiritual body. Paul says in 1 Corinthians 12, "Our bodies have many parts, but the many parts make up only one body when they are all put together. " So it is within the body of Christ. In verse 12, Paul goes on to say, "And some of the parts that seem weakest and least important are really the most necessary." Verse 22: "So

God has put the body together in such a way that extra honor and care are given to those parts that might otherwise seem less important." And in verse 24: "This makes for happiness among the parts, so that the parts have the same care for each other that they do for themselves. If one part suffers, all parts suffer with it, and if one part is honored, all the parts are glad."

Sometimes the foregoing principle is forgotten by the members and leaders of the church. Extra honor and care is not given to members who might otherwise be considered less important. Therefore, useful abilities, gifts, and talents are not exercised. This is especially true in the case of new members, who are usually babes in Christ, but who are on fire for God, and ready and willing to participate in the church in whatever capacity God leads them. It is the responsibility of the leaders, deacons, and elders of the church to utilize these members. If a new baby was restrained from physical exercise and healthy exploring, it would become discouraged, not develop, and would eventually die. So too, is this true when talents and abilities of new members are not allowed to be used in the church. The thrust too many times is to teach them the doctrine and traditions of the church. The member must prove that he or she can be a "good little" Baptist, Mormon, Lutheran, Presbyterian, Apostolic, Pentecostal, Church of God in Christ, Assemblies of God, etc. Leaders always justify this practice by comparing the church to a business whereby you are required to wear certain uniforms and have to learn that particular business' rules, regulations, and ways of doing things. This is understandable for leaders to look at it this way because in America we live in a capitalistic society. Something tells me Jesus was neither a capitalist nor a communist. He called his 12 disciples, trained them in the knowledge of God as best they could understand. He imparted knowledge and wisdom to them so that their raw abilities and talents could be fine-tuned over time and used so they could become "fishers" of men. Then he sent them out two by two. They were to teach what they had been taught and make other disciples.

The body became strong because of this exercise. Today, however, the church has other goals. It serves its own needs and its own self. Money is taken in through tithes and offerings and it is not always used to provide for the needs of the members nor the surrounding community, nor to further the work of the ministry, nor to support those working in the ministry. Some churches drain the energy, time, money, and consequently, the effectiveness of its body because they go to this church anniversary, that church anniversary, this pastoral anniversary, that pastoral anniversary, and district meetings, state meetings, and other weekly, monthly, and yearly functions within the local church, and other levels, that is, regional, statewide and international. Many times souls are not being reached or saved. The churches use these times to procure more monies from the already-drained church body.

The word of God is so vital and important to witnessing and sharing one's faith. Each member, whether an ordained minister, church officer, or church layman, can tell another how Christ has and still is working in his or her life. However slow of speech or inadequate a member may feel he is, with divine instruction from the Holy Spirit, and united in Christ with the rest of the body, others will note their boldness like that of Peter and John, and though "they perceived that they were unlearned and ignorant men, they marveled, and they took knowledge of them, that they had been with Jesus" (Acts 4:13).

Used and exercised daily, the new members of the body become proficient, polished, and more effective, and older members prolong their usefulness. With proper exercise, notice how the physical body takes on a healthy glow. The spiritual body, when witnessing, sharing the faith, ministering to the needs of others, too, takes on a healthy and vibrant tone – a flowing light shining before men "that they may see its (your) good works, and glorify your Father which is in Heaven" (Matt. 5:16). However, all parts of the body must be united in thought and effort. This doesn't mean everyone will be exactly the same. God doesn't deal with every individual in exactly the same way because He made each one unique and different and specially set each one apart for His service. However, all should work as a whole to be an effective witness to the world. Jesus prayed for all believers, thereby setting forth his goal for the church: "Neither pray I for these alone, but for them also which shall believe on me through their word; but for them also which shall believe on me through their word; that they all may be one; as you, Father, art in me, and I in you, that they also may be one in us; that the world may believe that you have sent me" (John 17:20-21).

Chapter 9. Cleaning Up Our Act

"Wash me thoroughly from my iniquity, and
cleanse me from my sin."
(Psalm 51:2)

The physical body requires daily cleansing to free itself of unhealthy external and internal impurities. But when cleansed, however thoroughly, with water alone, the physical body would not be completely clean. Soap, an important cleansing agent, must be added. So, too the spiritual body desperately needs daily cleansing with God's holy soap: the Holy Spirit. John said "I indeed baptize you with water, but there is one mightier than I, whose shoes I am unworthy to unloose, he will baptize you with the Holy Ghost, and with fire." (Matthew 3:11-12) When we are saved it is our spirit man who is saved, but it takes the Holy Ghost to work on that "soulish" area – those things that are in you like jealously, envy, backbiting, gossip, those little foxes that get us into trouble. Daily baptism of the Holy Spirit is the only means of cleansing "through and through." It produces righteousness and convicts of even the slightest and unknown sin. Spiritually, we may appear "clean," that is, we attend services, pay tithes and offerings, carry around expensive large Bibles, and even profess to love the Lord, that is, giving Him lip service while our hearts are far from Him. But the true test is manifested in works and actions. Do we truly love our brethren? Do we truly love those who are not saved enough to tell them about Christ? The Lord says "wherefore by their fruits ye shall know them." (Matthew 7:20)

The fire that John talks about is one of judgment. Fire is used to, among other things, cook food, harden pottery, and refine metals. Fire is one of the best purifiers. It takes all of the impurities out of meat. It's beyond me how most people can eat their meat rare or even medium rare. It is not only healthier to eat meat well done, but God told the Israelites they were not to eat or drink "the blood" or any animal because it would be impure and unclean for them. But the Holy Spirit takes us from a raw state where we have envy, anger, selfishness – all those symptoms of immaturity – to a mature or "well done" state. It is this state God wants us to attain. It is this state when he will say "well done" my good and faithful servant. Even God wants everything "well done."

Fire is also used to harden pottery. After the potter has molded and shaped the clay, that is, after God has shaped and molded us into what He wants us to be, we then have to be able "to stand." Pottery put into the kiln is a fiery test. The outer covering becomes hard, that is, that whole armor of God is not only baked into you, but becomes a part of your permanent covering. You can now stand against the wiles of the Devil and his forces.

Fire is used to refine metals. When metals are dipped in the boiling fiery water, the metals are cleansed and all of the dross starts to come to the surface. The dross, that includes impure thoughts, murmuring, and complaining, an impatient spirit, lack of control, and filthy and idle conversation. Once the dross comes up, that is it is recognized, not pushed down and hid – it must be skimmed off, a little at a time, or as much as can be taken off. This is a daily and ongoing process. More and more you will begin to shine and illuminate everyone you're around and everything you touch begins to prosper for God's purpose, not your own. What seems like defeat to others is actually victory in God's eyes. You become his humble and meek and most of all, loving servant. Your mind is renewed and transformed. You are cleaning up your act, and you have been "tried in the fire" and are now ready for the master's use.

If each member allowed God to do this refining process, the body of Christ would be effective in accomplishing the true goal which Jesus intended for His body: to be a light to a dying world so that souls are won to Him and finally reconciled back to God throughout all eternity.

Chapter 10. Rest and Re-Creation

*"And on the seventh day God ended His work which He had
done, and He rested on the seventh day from all His work which
He had done."*
(Genesis 2:2)

For the time being we are endowed with mortal bodies. These poor weak temporary "temples" eventually tire and must be restored and rejuvenated through rest, relaxation, and sleep at the end of a busy day. Each body is different and requires a different amount of rest, but an ample amount is necessary to awaken refreshed with the ability to function properly the next day. The necessary rest the spiritual body needs is true, earnest heart-searching prayer and meditation with God. Our Lord and Savior spent countless hours alone in prayer, thereby returning with an uplifted mind, a countenance of peace, His heart at rest, and renewed with freshness and power. Sometimes in the daily life, we get so busy and active – guided primarily by the time clock – working fervently to meet almost impossible deadlines – that we slowly neglect the needed time for rest, eventually trying to get by on less and less, forcing the body to function and stay awake through unnatural means such as stimulants and drugs. The body rapidly wears out due to such continued abuse, and is no longer fit for the service for which it was intended. For example, after 24 hours without proper rest, the body begins to function less capably. After about 10 sleepless days, the body has trouble carrying out mental and physical tasks, and the judgment and memory deteriorates. If kept awake long enough the person may hallucinate and show signs of mental illness. Also, this tends to break down willpower and to make one less vigilant and more suggestible – often to negative forces.

So too, the same effects can be realized in the spiritual body when prayer, meditation, and worship are neglected. This time must be spent at home personally with God and should be spent at times with other members of the body for support and strength. Lack of spiritual discernment is life-threatening, and without this vital communication with the divine, the willpower is broken down, making the spiritual body helplessly susceptible to Satan's wiles and temptations. Neglected prayer is also evident in the lack of zeal for God and love for fallen humanity. We attend services with dead, lifeless, and worn out souls, who are suffering under heavy burdens and still holding onto past grudges. They are still harboring secret sins and hatred of which should have been repented. Also, we should be shedding our will for God's will, as did Christ, our example, in the Garden of Gethsemane. Had we spent the necessary time in prayer (communion with God alone has all the answers and the ability to lift us up above the cares of the world), our minds would be alive and refreshed, ready to discern and put into practice, spiritual truths presented to us.

It is important for the members of the body to unite together at least once a week for Prayer Meeting. These meetings should be not only instructional, but inspirational as well, allowing all present to participate and share burdens, blessings, and even confessing sins. The Bible says that in these days we should not only "watch and pray," but Paul exhorts us to not "worry about anything, instead pray about everything, tell God your needs and don't forget to thank him for his answers" (Phil. 4:6-7). This will produce the rest and peace of mind.

And lastly, but not least, most would prefer to think of time away from work as recreation, but our Lord reveres it as a memorial day of "re-creation." This day at the end of the tiring workweek is vital to the spiritual body's survival. The Lord says, "The Sabbath was made for man and not man for the Sabbath" (Mark 2:27). Therefore, it is a privilege to wholeheartedly partake of something made exclusively for you. We look forward to following the Creator's example toward rejuvenation, who said of the Sabbath: "It is a sign between me and the children of Israel (now us) forever: for in six days the Lord made heaven and earth, and on the seventh day he rested" and was refreshed (Exodus 31:16-17). Even though the psalmist says "I was glad when they said unto me, let us go into the house of the Lord" (Psalm 122:1), and many talk about going and lifting up our hands in the sanctuary, and "I would rather be a doorkeeper in the house of my God, than to dwell in the tents of wickedness" (Psalm 84:10), one must understand that because of the Holy Spirit dwelling within us, we are the temple of the Lord (1 Corinthians 3:16). Where we go therein is the church. We still need other believers. We still need to congregate and assemble with each other, not out of form and fashion, or tradition and formality, but with heartfelt worship. The Lord says "where two or more are gathered in my name, there I am in the midst" (Matt. 18:20) Most denounce and put down televangelists and home worship, but once again we are not rightly dividing the word of God and taking into account how times and technology have evolved since the Bible was written. God gave us His Holy Spirit to lead us into all truth. He does not want us to be ignorant, because He says "my people perish for lack of knowledge" (Hosea 4:6). In Biblical days, there were no technological modes of communication and transportation, no computers, like today. Believe it or not, two believers can have "church on the phone." It is your desire and your heart God is concerned with. We must let the Spirit of God "burn away" that narrow-minded and judgmental spirit, like that of the Pharisees and Sadducees of Christ's day. We must forgive those who cried out "crucify him!"

Chapter 11. Diagnosis – 30-for-30

*"Those who are well have no need of a physician
but those who are sick." (Matt. 9:12b)*

Monthly (30-day) Test for Your Ministry Progression & Effectiveness

As a Christian and child of the Most High God, we each should do a regular check-up of how we are doing spiritually, how we are progressing within our ministry and/or calling, and how effective we are as Christians. The check-up should be done once a month, analyzed, and reviewed. After this, the conviction of the Holy Spirit should prompt us to work on our weaknesses and allow the Lord to prune us even in those areas in which we think we excel.

Attached is the checklist. It should be noted that this is a self-assessment. You should make 12 copies (one for each month of the year). The left column contains the 30 spiritual areas of concern. The middle column is for diagnosis purposes and for scoring. The right column is for treatment and indicates the recommended amount of time needed.

Spiritual Area		Diagnosis										Prescription Time Span (in days)			
		Chronic			Acute			Healthy			P	7	14	21	30
1	Continually in a spirit of prayer	1	2	3	4	5	6	7	8	9	10				
2	Reading my word daily.	1	2	3	4	5	6	7	8	9	10				
3	Studying my word daily.	1	2	3	4	5	6	7	8	9	10				
4	Patiently waiting on God	1	2	3	4	5	6	7	8	9	10				
5	Fasting when the Lord ordains it – and knowing how to fast	1	2	3	4	5	6	7	8	9	10				
6	Planning but allowing God to lead and establish those plans	1	2	3	4	5	6	7	8	9	10				
7	Witnessing on a regular basis	1	2	3	4	5	6	7	8	9	10				
8	Drawing others with the chords of love	1	2	3	4	5	6	7	8	9	10				
9	Allowing self to die daily	1	2	3	4	5	6	7	8	9	10				
10	Depending and relying on God (totally)	1	2	3	4	5	6	7	8	9	10				
11	Endeavoring to be the best person I can be	1	2	3	4	5	6	7	8	9	10				
12	Love God with heart, mind, and soul, that is, in word and in deed	1	2	3	4	5	6	7	8	9	10				
13	Giving time, money, and resources for God's work	1	2	3	4	5	6	7	8	9	10				
14	Having an obedient and teachable spirit	1	2	3	4	5	6	7	8	9	10				
15	Show respect and love to everyone	1	2	3	4	5	6	7	8	9	10				

	Spiritual Area	Diagnosis											Prescription Time Span (in days)			
		Chronic			Acute			Healthy			P		7	14	21	30
16	Love others as I love myself	1	2	3	4	5	6	7	8	9	10					
17	Love myself	1	2	3	4	5	6	7	8	9	10					
18	Respect myself	1	2	3	4	5	6	7	8	9	10					
19	Dress, talk, walk, and carry myself as a servant of God	1	2	3	4	5	6	7	8	9	10					
20	Follow through on all that I am given to do and do it all to the glory of God	1	2	3	4	5	6	7	8	9	10					
21	Don't complain – ask questions	1	2	3	4	5	6	7	8	9	10					
22	Don't gossip – ask no questions	1	2	3	4	5	6	7	8	9	10					
23	Always a willing worker	1	2	3	4	5	6	7	8	9	10					
24	Working on developing all Fruit of the Sprit	1	2	3	4	5	6	7	8	9	10					
25	Hate sin – run, not tiptoe away from it	1	2	3	4	5	6	7	8	9	10					
26	Primary goal is to see souls saved and stay saved	1	2	3	4	5	6	7	8	9	10					
27	Don't backstab – seek to remove the knife and heal the wound	1	2	3	4	5	6	7	8	9	10					
28	Have a meek and humble spirit	1	2	3	4	5	6	7	8	9	10					
29	Praise and worship God in spirit and in truth	1	2	3	4	5	6	7	8	9	10					
30	Saved, filled with the Holy Ghost	0	There is no middle ground for this area – either you are or you are not!								10					

139

Chapter 12. Treatment

"Physician, heal thyself." (Luke 4:23b)

Treatment should be applied to one spiritual area at a time. A

suggestion for treatment is as follows:

Score	Indicator	Treatment Time
1 – 3	Chronic	All 7 scriptures daily for 30 days
4 – 6	Acute	4-5 scriptures daily for 21 days
7 – 9	Healthy	2-3 scriptures daily for 14 days
10	Pretty Near Perfect	1 scripture daily for 7 days for healthy maintenance – pruning

1 – Continually in a spirit of prayer

Psalm 55:17   Evening, and morning, and at noon, will I pray, and cry aloud: and He shall hear my voice.

Psalm 5:1-3   Give ear to my words, O Lord, consider my mediation. Hearken unto the voice of my cry, my King, and my God: for unto you will I pray. My voice shall you hear in the morning, O Lord; in the morning will I direct my prayer unto you, and will look up.

Prov. 15:29   The Lord is far from the wicked: but He hears the prayer of the righteous.

Isaiah 55:6   Seek the Lord while He may be found, call upon Him while He is near.

Rom. 12:12   Rejoicing in hope; patient in tribulation; continuing instant in prayer.

Ephes. 6:18   Praying always with all prayer and supplication in the Spirit, and watching therein with all perseverance and supplication for all saints.

Jude 20   But you, beloved, building up yourselves on your most holy faith, praying in the Holy Ghost.

2 – Reading my word daily

Deut. 6:5-9   And you shall love the LORD thy God with all your heart, and with all your soul, and with all your might. And these words, which I command you this day, shall be in your heart: and you shall teach them diligently unto thy children, and shall talk of them when you sit in your house, and when you walk by the way, and when you lie down, and when you rise up. And you shall bind them for a sign upon your hand, and they shall be as frontlets between your eyes. And you shall write them upon the posts of your house, and on your gates.

Josh 1:8   This book of the law shall not depart out of your mouth; but you shall meditate therein day and night, that you may observe to do according to all that is written therein: for then you shall make your way prosperous, and then you shall have good success.

John 1:1   In the beginning was the Word, and the Word was with God, and the Word was God.

Heb. 4:12   For the word of God is quick, and powerful, and sharper than any two-edged sword, piercing even to the dividing asunder of soul and spirit, and of the joints and marrow, and is a discerner of the thoughts and intents of the heart.

2 Timothy 3:16

All scripture is given by inspiration of God, and is profitable for doctrine, for reproof, for correction, for instruction in righteousness: that the man of God may be perfect, completely furnished unto all good works

2 Peter 1:20   Knowing this first, that no prophecy of the scripture is of any private interpretation.

Rev. 1:3   Blessed is he that reads, and they that hear the words of this prophecy, and keep those things which are written therein: for the time is at hand.

3 – Studying my word daily

James 1:21-23 Therefore, ridding yourselves of all moral filth and evil excess, humbly receive the implanted word, which is able to save you. But be doers of the word and not hearers only, deceiving yourselves. Because if anyone is a hearer of the word and not a doer, he is like a man looking at his own face in a mirror;

Heb 6:5   And have tasted the good word of God, and the powers of the world to come.

1 Peter 2:2   As newborn babes, desire the sincere milk of the word, that ye may grow thereby

Luke 11:28	But he said, Yea rather, blessed are they that hear the word of God, and keep it.
James 1:18	Of his own will begat he us with the word of truth, that we should be a kind of firstfruits of his creatures.
Phil. 2:16	Holding forth the word of life; that I may rejoice in the day of Christ, that I have not run in vain, neither labor in vain.
Ephes. 6:17	And take the helmet of salvation, and the sword of the Spirit, which is the word of God.

4 – Patiently waiting on God

Luke 21:19	In your patience possess you your souls.
Heb. 10:36	For you have need of patience, that, after you have done the will of God, you might receive the promise.
James 1:2-3	My brethren, count it all joy when you fall into divers temptations; Knowing this, that the trying of your faith works patience.
1 Peter 2:20	For what glory is it, if, when you are buffeted for your faults, you shall take it patiently? but if, when you do well, and suffer for it, you take it patiently, this is acceptable with God.
Prov. 16:32	He that is slow to anger is better than the mighty; and he that rules his spirit than he that takes a city.
Isaiah 30:15b	. . . in quietness and in confidence shall be your strength: and you would not.

5 – Fasting when the Lord ordains it – and knowing how to fast

Isaiah 58:4-6	Behold, you fast for strife and debate, and to smite with the fist of wickedness: you shall not fast as you do this day, to make your voice to be heard on high. Is it such a fast that I have chosen? a day for a man to afflict his soul? is it to bow down his head as a bulrush, and to spread sackcloth and ashes under him? Will you call this a fast, and an acceptable day

to the LORD? Is not this the fast that I have chosen? to loose the bands of wickedness, to undo the heavy burdens, and to let the oppressed go free, and that you break every yoke?

Matt. 6:16-18   When the even was come, they brought unto him many that were possessed with devils: and he cast out the spirits with his word, and healed all that were sick: That it might be fulfilled which was spoken by Esaias the prophet, saying, Himself took our infirmities, and bare our sicknesses. Now when Jesus saw great multitudes about him, he gave commandment to depart unto the other side.

Rom. 14:21   It is good neither to eat flesh, nor to drink wine, nor any thing whereby your brother stumbles, or is offended, or is made weak.

Luke 4:2   Being forty days tempted of the devil. And in those days he did eat nothing: and when they were ended, he afterward hungered.

Acts 14:23   And when they had ordained them elders in every church, and had prayed with fasting, they commended them to the Lord, on whom they believed.

Luke 18:12   I fast twice in the week, I give tithes of all that I possess.

Jer. 14:12   When they fast, I will not hear their cry; and when they offer burnt offering and an oblation, I will not accept them: but I will consume them by the sword, and by the famine, and by the pestilence.

6 – Planning but allowing God to lead and establish those plans

Romans 1:13   Now I would not have you ignorant, brethren, that oftentimes I purposed to come unto you, (but was let hitherto,) that I might have some fruit among you also, even as among other Gentiles.

Heb. 11:1   Now faith is the substance of things hoped for, the evidence of things not seen.

James 4:13-15 Go to now, ye that say, To day or to morrow we will go into such a city, and continue there a year, and buy and sell, and get gain: Whereas ye know not what shall be on the morrow. For what is your life? It is even a vapor, that appears for a little time, and then vanishes away. For that ye ought to say, If the Lord will, we shall live, and do this, or that.

Eccl. 3:11 He hath made every thing beautiful in his time: also he hath set the world in their heart, so that no man can find out the work that God makes from the beginning to the end.

Psalms 90:12 So teach us to number our days, that we may apply our hearts unto wisdom.

Ephes. 4:16 From whom the whole body fitly joined together and compacted by that which every joint supplies, according to the effectual working in the measure of every part, makes increase of the body unto the edifying of itself in love.

1 Chr. 28:19 All this, said David, the LORD made me understand in writing by his hand upon me, even all the works of this pattern.

1 Cor. 13:12 For now we see through a glass, darkly; but then face to face: now I know in part; but then shall I know even as also I am known.

7 – Witnessing on a regular basis

1 Thess. 2:5 For neither at any time used we flattering words, as ye know, nor a cloak of covetousness; God is witness.

John 7:5 For neither did his brethren believe in him.

James 2:2 For if there come unto your assembly a man with a gold ring, in goodly apparel, and there come in also a poor man in vile raiment.

Acts 1:6-8 When they therefore were come together, they asked of him, saying, Lord, wilt thou at this time restore again the kingdom to Israel? And he said unto them, It is not for you to know the times or the seasons, which the Father hath put in his own power. But ye shall receive power, after that the Holy Ghost is come upon you: and ye shall be witnesses unto me both in Jerusalem, and in all Judaea, and in Samaria, and unto the uttermost part of the earth.

John 1:5 — And the light shines in darkness; and the darkness comprehended it not.

1 John 1:8-10 — If we say that we have no sin, we deceive ourselves, and the truth is not in us. If we confess our sins, he is faithful and just to forgive us our sins, and to cleanse us from all unrighteousness. If we say that we have not sinned, we make him a liar, and his word is not in us.

John 4:5-7 — Then cometh he to a city of Samaria, which is called Sychar, near to the parcel of ground that Jacob gave to his son Joseph. Now Jacob's well was there. Jesus therefore, being wearied with his journey, sat thus on the well: and it was about the sixth hour. There cometh a woman of Samaria to draw water: Jesus said unto her, Give me to drink.

8 – Drawing others with the chords of love

Rom. 13:8-10 — Owe no man anything, but to love one another: for he that loves another hath fulfilled the law. For this, Thou will not commit adultery, Thou will not kill, Thou will not steal, Thou will not bear false witness, Thou will not covet; and if there be any other commandment, it is briefly comprehended in this saying, namely, Thou will love thy neighbor as thyself. Love works no ill to his neighbor: therefore love is the fulfilling of the law.

John 13:34 — A new commandment I give unto you, That you love one another; as I have loved you, that you also love one another.

1 Cor. 13:4-8   Charity suffers long, and is kind; charity envies not; charity vaunts not itself, is not puffed up, Does not behave itself unseemly, seeks not her own, is not easily provoked, thinks no evil; Rejoices not in iniquity, but rejoices in the truth; Bears all things, believeth all things, hopes all things, endures all things. Charity never fails: but whether there be prophecies, they shall fail; whether there be tongues, they shall cease; whether there be knowledge, it shall vanish away.

Matt. 22:37-39 Jesus said unto him, you will love the Lord your God with all your heart, and with all your soul, and with all your mind. This is the first and great commandment. And the second is like unto it, you will love thy neighbor as yourself.

Matt. 7:12   Therefore all things whatsoever you would that men should do to you, do you even so to them: for this is the law and the prophets.

Prov. 10:12   Hatred stirs up strife: but love covers all sins.

Rom. 13:8   Owe no man any thing, but to love one another: for he that loves another hath fulfilled the law.

9 – Allowing self to die daily

Psalms 39:7-13

And now, Lord, what wait I for? my hope is in thee. Deliver me from all my transgressions: make me not the reproach of the foolish. I was dumb, I opened not my mouth; because thou didst it. Remove thy stroke away from me: I am consumed by the blow of your hand. When thou with rebukes dost correct man for iniquity, you make his beauty to consume away like a moth: surely every man is vanity. Selah. Hear my prayer, O LORD, and give ear unto my cry; hold not thy peace at my tears: for I am a stranger with thee, and a sojourner, as all my fathers were. O spare me, that I may recover strength, before I go hence, and be no more.

Palms 103:3   Who forgives all your iniquities; who heals all your diseases.

Amos 6:8   The Lord GOD hath sworn by himself, says the LORD the God of hosts, I abhor the excellency of Jacob, and hate his palaces: therefore will I deliver up the city with all that is therein.

Eccl. 2:11   Then I looked on all the works that my hands had wrought, and on the labor that I had labored to do: and, behold, all was vanity and vexation of spirit, and there was no profit under the sun.

Matt. 13:22   He also that received seed among the thorns is he that hears the word; and the care of this world, and the deceitfulness of riches, choke the word, and he becomes unfruitful.

Rev. 18:3   For all nations have drunk of the wine of the wrath of her fornication, and the kings of the earth have committed fornication with her, and the merchants of the earth are waxed rich through the abundance of her delicacies.

James 3:8   But the tongue can no man tame; it is an unruly evil, full of deadly poison.

10 – Depending and relying on God (totally)

Gen. 50:20   But as for you, ye thought evil against me; but God meant it unto good, to bring to pass, as it is this day, to save much people alive.

Prov. 4:25-26   Let your eyes look right on, and let your eyelids look straight before you. Ponder the path of your feet, and let all your ways be established.

Prov. 3:5-6   Trust in the LORD with all your heart; and lean not unto your own understanding. In all your ways acknowledge him, and he shall direct your paths.

Psalm 8:4-6   What is man, that thou art mindful of him? and the son of man, that thou visits him? For thou hast made him a little lower than the angels, and hast crowned him with glory and honor. You made him to have dominion over the works of your hands; you hast put all things under his feet:

Psalm 46:1-3   God is our refuge and strength, a very present help in trouble. Therefore will not we fear, though the earth be removed, and though the mountains be carried into the midst of the sea; Though the waters thereof roar and be troubled, though the mountains shake with the swelling thereof. Selah.

Psalm 91:4   He will cover you with his feathers, and under his wings will you trust: his truth shall be your shield and buckler.

Heb. 13:5-6   Let your conversation be without covetousness; and be content with such things as you have: for he has said, I will never leave you, nor forsake you. So that we may boldly say, The Lord is my helper, and I will not fear what man will do to me.

11 – Endeavoring to be the best I can be

1 Cor. 3:9-15   For we are laborers together with God: ye are God's husbandry, ye are God's building. According to the grace of God which is given unto me, as a wise master-builder, I have laid the foundation, and another builds thereon. But let every man take heed how he builds thereupon. For other foundation can no man lay than that is laid, which is Jesus Christ. Now if any man build upon this foundation gold, silver, precious stones, wood, hay, stubble; Every man's work shall be made manifest: for the day shall declare it, because it shall be revealed by fire; and the fire shall try every man's work of what sort it is. If any man's work abide which he hath built thereupon, he shall receive a reward. If any man's work shall be burned, he shall suffer loss: but he himself shall be saved; yet so as by fire.

1 Cor. 3:13-15 Every man's work shall be made manifest: for the day shall declare it, because it shall be revealed by fire; and the fire shall try every man's work of what

sort it is. If any man's work abide which he hath built thereupon, he shall receive a reward. If any man's work shall be burned, he shall suffer loss: but he himself shall be saved; yet so as by fire.

Ephes. 5:2-5   And walk in love, as Christ also hath loved us, and hath given himself for us an offering and a sacrifice to God for a sweet-smelling savor. But fornication, and all uncleanness, or covetousness, let it not be once named among you, as becomes saints; Neither filthiness, nor foolish talking, nor jesting, which are not convenient: but rather giving of thanks. For this ye know, that no whoremonger, nor unclean person, nor covetous man, who is an idolater, hath any inheritance in the kingdom of Christ and of God.

Ephes. 5:16   Redeeming the time, because the days are evil.

John 15:5-6   Yes, I am the vine; you are the branches. Those who remain in me, and I in them, will produce much fruit. For apart from me you can do nothing.

1 Cor. 10:31   Whether therefore ye eat, or drink, or whatsoever ye do, do all to the glory of God.

Prov. 28:13   People who cover over their sins will not prosper. But if they confess and forsake them, they will receive mercy.

Psalm 51:1-10 Have mercy on me, O God, because of your unfailing love. Because of your great compassion, blot out the stain of my sins. Wash me clean from my guilt. Purify me from my sins. For I recognize my shameful deeds – they haunt me day and night. Against you, and you alone, have I sinned; I have done what is evil in your sight. You will be proved right in what you say, and your judgment against me is just. For I was born a sinner – yes, from the moment my mother conceived me. But you desire honesty from the heart, so you can teach me to be wise in my inmost being. Purify me from my sins, and I will be clean; wash me, and I will be whiter than snow. Oh, give me back my joy again; you have broken me – now let me rejoice. Don't keep looking at my sins. Remove the stain of my guilt. Create in me a clean heart, O God. Renew a right spirit within me.

12 – Love God with heart, mind, and soul, that is, in word and in deed

Psalm 91:14-16

The Lord says, "I will rescue those who love me. I will protect those who trust in my name. When they call on me, I will answer; I will be with them in trouble. I will rescue them and honor them. I will satisfy them with a long life and give them my salvation.

Mark 12:29-30 The most important commandment is this: "Hear, O Israel! The Lord our God is the one and only Lord. And you must love the Lord your God with all your heart, all your soul, all your mind, and all your strength."

John 14:15-16 Those who obey my commandments are the ones who love me. And because they love me, my Father will love them, and I will love them. And I will reveal myself to each one of them.

1 Cor. 2:9 No eye has seen, no ear has heard, and no mind has imagined what God has prepared for those who love him.

1 John 4:20 If someone says, "I love God," but hates another Christian, that person is a liar; for if we don't love people we can see, how can we love God, whom we have not seen?

1 Cor. 8:1-3 While knowledge may make us feel important, it is love that really builds up the church. Anyone who claims to know all the answers doesn't really know very much. But the person who loves God is the one God knows and cares for.

Deut. 10:12 And now, Israel, what does the LORD your God require of you, but to fear the LORD your God, to walk in all his ways, and to love him, and to serve the LORD your God with all your heart and with all your soul.

13 – Giving time, money, and resources for God's work

Prov. 3:9-10   Honour the LORD with your substance, and with the firstfruits of all your increase: So shall your barns be filled with plenty, and your presses shall burst out with new wine.

Matt. 16:26   How do you benefit if you gain the whole world but lose your own soul in the process?   Is anything worth more than your soul?

1 Cor. 7:31   Those in frequent contact with the things of the world should make good use of them without become attached to them, for this world and all it contains will pass away.

Deut. 14:27-29 And the Levite that is within your gates; you will not forsake him; for he has no part nor inheritance with you. At the end of three years you will bring forth all the tithe of your increase the same year, and will lay it up within your gates: And the Levite, (because he hath no part nor inheritance with you,) and the stranger, and the fatherless, and the widow, which are within your gates, shall come, and shall eat and be satisfied; that the LORD your God may bless you in all the work of your hand which you do.

Matt. 5:17-20   Think not that I am come to destroy the law, or the prophets: I am not come to destroy, but to fulfill. For verily I say unto you, Till heaven and earth pass, one jot or one tittle shall in no wise pass from the law, till all be fulfilled. Whosoever therefore shall break one of these least commandments, and shall teach men so, he shall be called the least in the kingdom of heaven: but whosoever shall do and teach them, the same shall be called great in the kingdom of heaven. For I say unto you, That except your righteousness shall exceed the righteousness of the scribes and Pharisees, ye shall in no case enter into the kingdom of heaven.

1 Cor. 9:13-14 Do ye not know that they which minister about holy things live of the things of the temple? and they which wait at the altar are partakers with the altar? Even so hath the Lord ordained that they which preach the gospel should live of the gospel.

Gal. 6:6 Let him that is taught in the word communicate unto him that teaches in all good things.

14 – Having an obedient and teachable spirit

Rom 8:7-9 The sinful nature is always hostile to God. It never did obey God's laws, and it never will. That's why those who are still under the control of their sinful nature can never please God. But you are not controlled by your sinful nature. You are controlled by the Spirit if you have the Spirit of God living in you.

Psalm 119:2 Happy are those who obey his decrees and search for him with all their hearts.

Matt. 7:24 Anyone who listens to my teaching and obeys me is wise, like a person who builds a house on solid rock.

Phil. 4:9 Keep putting into practice all you learned from me and heard from me and saw me doing, and the God of peace will be with you.

Matt. 7:21 Not all people who sound religious are really godly. They may refer to me as "Lord," but they still won't enter the Kingdom of Heaven. The decisive issue is whether they obey my Father in heaven.

Rom. 6:16 Don't you realize that whatever you choose to obey becomes your master? You can choose sin, which leads to death, or you can choose to obey God and receive his approval.

1 Sam 15:22 Has the Lord as great delight in burnt offering and sacrifices, as in obeying the voice of the Lord?

> Behold, to obey is better than sacrifice, And to heed than the fat of rams.

15 – Show respect and love to everyone

Rom. 12:14,20

> If people persecute you because you are a Christian, don't curse them; pray that God will bless them. Instead, do what the Scriptures say: "If your enemies are hungry, feed them. If they are thirsty, give them something to drink, and they will be ashamed of what they have done to you."

Matt. 5:43

> You have heard the law of Moses says, "Love your neighbor" and hate your enemy. But I say, love your enemies! Pray for those who persecute you! In that way, you will be acting as true children of your Father in heaven.

Prov. 24:17-18

> Do not rejoice when your enemies fall into trouble. Don't be happy then they stumble. For the Lord will be displeased with you and will turn his anger away from them.

1 Cor. 1:10

> Now I plead with you, brethren, by the name of our Lord Jesus Christ, that you all speak the same thing, and that there be no divisions among you, but that you be perfectly joined together in the same mind and in the same judgment.

1 Cor. 8:9

> But beware lest somehow this liberty of yours become a stumbling block to those who are weak.

1 Cor. 9:19a

> For though I am free from all men, I have made myself a servant to all, that I might win the more.

1 Cor. 14:26

> How is it then, brethren? Whenever you come together, each of you has a psalm, has a teaching, has a tongue, has a revelation, has an interpretation. Let all things be done for edification.

16 – Love others as I love myself

John 15:12   This is my commandment, that ye love one another, as I have loved you.

Rom. 12:10   Be kindly affectionate one to another with brotherly love; in honor preferring one another.

Gal 5:13b-15   ... by love serve one another. For all the law is fulfilled in one word, even in this; You shall love thy neighbor as thyself. But if ye bite and devour one another, take heed that ye be not consumed one of another.

Col. 2:2   That their hearts might be comforted, being knit together in love ...

Col. 3:13-14   Forbearing one another, and forgiving one another, if any man have a quarrel against any; even as Christ forgave you, so also do ye. And above all things put on charity, which is the bond of perfection.

1 Thess. 3:12-13

                And the Lord make you to increase and abound in love one toward another, and toward all men, even as we do toward you: to the end he may establish your hearts not "unblameable" in holiness before God, even our Father, at the coming of our Lord Jesus Christ with all his saints.

1 John 4:7,8   Beloved, let us love one another: for love is of God; and everyone that loves is born of God, and knows God. He that loves not knows not God; for God is love.

17 – Love myself

Genesis 1:31   Then God saw everything that He had made, and indeed it was very good.

Matt. 10:29-31 Not even a sparrow, worth only half a penny, can fall to the ground without your Father knowing it. And the very hairs on your head are all numbered. So don't be afraid; you are more valuable to him than a whole flock of sparrows.

Matt. 5:13-16   You are the salt of the earth. But what good is salt if it has lost its flavor? Can you make it useful again? It will be thrown out and trampled underfoot as worthless. You are the light of the world – like a city on a mountain, glowing in the night for all to see. Don't hide your light under a basket! Instead, put it on a stand and let it shine for all. In the same way, let your good deeds shine out for all to see, so that everyone will praise your heavenly Father.

Rom 12:3-6   As God's messenger, I give each of you this warning: Be honest in your estimate of yourselves, measuring your value by how much faith God has given you. Just as our bodies have many parts and each part has a special function, so it is with Christ's body. We are all parts of his one body, and each of us has different work to do. And since we are all one body in Christ, we belong to each other, and each of us needs all the others. God has given each of us the ability to do certain things well.

2 Cor. 10:17-18   As the Scriptures say, "The person who wishes to boast should boast only of what the Lord has done." When people boast about themselves, it doesn't count for much. But when the Lord commends someone, that's different!

2 Cor. 12:7-8   I have received wonderful revelations from God. But to keep me from getting puffed up, I was given a thorn in my flesh, a messenger from Satan to torment me and keep me from getting proud. Three different times I begged the Lord to take it away. Each time he said, "My gracious favor is all you need. My power works best in your weakness,"

1 Peter 2:9-10   You are a chosen people. You are a kingdom of priests, God's holy nation, his very own possession. This is so you can show others the goodness of God, for he called you out of the darkness into his wonderful light. "Once you were not a people; now you are the people of God. Once you received none of God's mercy; now you have received his mercy."

18 – Respect myself

Prov. 26:23-26 Smooth words may hide a wicked heart, just as a pretty glaze, covers a common clay pot. People with hate in their hearts may sound pleasant enough, but don't believe them. Though they pretend to be kind, their hearts are full of all kinds of evil. While their hatred may be concealed by trickery, it will finally come to light for all to see.

Phil 1:20 According to my earnest expectation and my hope, that in nothing I shall be ashamed, but that with all boldness, as always, so now also Christ shall be magnified in my body, whether it be by life, or by death.

Prov. 28:1b ... but the righteous are bold as a lion.

Psalm 138:6 Though the Lord be high, yet hath He respect unto the lowly; but the proud He knows afar off.

Psalm 56:4 I trust in God, so why should I be afraid? What can mere mortals do to me?

Matt. 5:13-16 You are the salt of the earth. But what good is salt if it has lost its flavor? Can you make it useful again? It will be thrown out and trampled underfoot as worthless. You are the light of the world – like a city on a mountain, glowing in the night for all to see. Don't hide your light under a basket! Instead, put it on a stand and let it shine for all. In the same way, let your good deeds shine out for all to see, so that everyone will praise your heavenly Father.

1 Peter 2:9 You are a chosen people. You are a kingdom of priests, God's holy nation, his very own possession. This is so you can show others the goodness of God, for he called you out of the darkness into his wonderful light.

19 – Dress, talk, walk, and carry myself as a servant of God

Matt. 16:24 Jesus said to the disciples, "If any of you wants to be my follower, you must put aside your selfish ambition, shoulder your cross, and follow me.

Luke 6:31-36   Do for others as you would like them to do for you. Do you think you deserve credit merely for loving those who love you? Even the sinners do that? And if you do good only to those who do good to you, is that so wonderful? Even sinners do that much! And if you lend money only to those who can repay you, what good is that? Even sinners will lend to their own kind for a full return. Love your enemies! Do good to them! Lend to them! And don't be concerned that they might not repay. Then your reward from heaven will be very great, and you will truly be acting as children of the Most High, for he is kind to the unthankful and to those who are wicked. You must be compassionate, just as your Father is compassionate.

Ephes. 4:2-3   Be humble and gentle. Be patient with each other, making allowance for each other's faults because of your love. Always keep yourselves united in the Holy Spirit, and bind yourselves together with peace.

Phil. 2:3-5   Don't be selfish, don't live to make a good impression on others. Be humble, thinking of others as better than yourself. Don't think only about your own affairs, but be interested in others, too, and what they are doing. Your attitude should be the same that Christ Jesus had.

1 John 3:10   Anyone who does not obey God's commands and does not love other Christians does not belong to God.

Prov. 20:14, 23

The buyer haggles over the price, saying, "It's worthless," then brags about getting a bargain! The Lord despises double standards; he is not pleased by dishonest scales.

Gal. 5:22-25   When the Holy Spirit controls our lives, he will produce this kind of fruit in us: love, joy, peace, patience, kindness, goodness, faithfulness, gentleness, and self-control. Here there is no conflict with the law. Those who belong to Christ Jesus have nailed the passions and desires of their sinful nature to his cross and crucified them there. If we are living now by the Holy Spirit, let us follow

20 – Follow through on all that I am given to do and do it all to the glory of God

Psalm 139:1-5 O Lord, you have examined my heart and know everything about me. You know when I sit down or stand up. You know my every thought when far away. You chart the path ahead of me and tell me where to stop and rest. Every moment you know where I am. You know what I am going to say even before I say it, Lord. You both precede and follow me. You place your hand of blessing on my head.

Exodus 15:26 And said, If thou wilt diligently hearken to the voice of the Lord thy God, and wilt do that which is right in his sight, and wilt give ear to his commandments, and keep all his statutes, I will put none of these diseases upon thee, which I have brought upon the Egyptians: for I am the Lord that healeth thee.

Joshua 22:5 But take diligent heed to do the commandment and the law, which Moses the servant of the Lord charged you, to love the Lord your God, and to walk in all his ways, and to keep his commandments, and to cleave unto him, and to serve him with all your heart and with all your soul.

Proverbs 21:5

The thoughts of the diligent tend only to plenteousness; but of every one that is hasty only to want.

Proverbs 22:29

Seest thou a man diligent in his business? he shall stand before kings; he shall not stand before mean men.

Luke 15:8   Either what woman having ten pieces of silver, if she lose one piece, doth not light a candle, and sweep the house, and seek diligently till she find it?

1 Timothy 5:10

Well reported of for good works; if she have brought up children, if she have lodged strangers, if she have washed the saints' feet, if she have relieved the afflicted, if she have diligently followed every good work.

21 – Don't complain – ask questions

Psalm 55:22   Cast your burden upon the Lord, and He will sustain you: He will never allow the righteous to be moved.

Phil 4:6   Be worried about nothing, but in everything by prayer and supplication with thanksgiving, let your requests be made known unto God.

Prov. 17:22   A cheerful heart is good medicine, but a broken spirit saps a person's strength.

1 Tim. 6:6-8   True religion with contentment is great wealth. After all, we didn't bring anything with us when we came into the world, and we certainly cannot carry anything with us when we die. So if we have enough food and clothing, let us be content.

Prov. 23:17-18 Don't envy sinners, but always continue to fear the Lord. For surely you have a future ahead of you; your hope will not be disappointed.

Phil. 4:11-13 I have learned how to get along happily whether I have much or little. I know how to live on almost nothing or with everything. I have learned the secret of living in every situation, whether it is with a full stomach or empty, with plenty or little. For I can do everything with the help of Christ who gives me the strength I need.

Eccles. 5:12   Enjoy what you have rather than desiring what you don't have. Just dreaming about nice things is meaningless; it is like chasing the wind.

22 – Don't gossip – ask no questions

1 Sam. 16:7	The Lord doesn't make decisions the way you do! People judge by outward appearance, but the Lord looks at a person's thoughts and intentions.
Matt. 7:1-5	Stop judging others, and you will not be judged. For others will treat you as you treat them. Whatever measure you use in judging others, it will be used to measure how you are judged. And why worry about a speck in your friend's eye when you have a log in your own? How can you think of saying, "Friend, let me help you get rid of that speck in your eye," when you can't see past the log in your own eye? Hypocrite! First get rid of the log from your own eye; then perhaps you will see well enough to deal with the speck in your fiend's eye.
James 4:11-12	Don't speak evil against each other, my dear brothers and sisters. If you criticize each other and condemn each other, then you are criticizing and condemning God's law. But you are not a judge who can decide whether the law is right or wrong. Your job is to obey it. God alone, who made the law, can rightly judge among us. He alone has the power to save or to destroy. So what right do you have to condemn your neighbor?
Psalm 34:12-15	
	Do any of you want to live a life that is long and good? Then watch your tongue! Keep your lips from telling lies! Turn away from evil and do good. Work hard at living in peace with others. The eyes of the Lord watch over those who do right; his ears are open to their cries for help.
Prov. 11:12-13	It is foolish to belittle a neighbor; a person with good sense remains silent. A gossip goes around revealing secrets, but those who are trustworthy can keep a confidence.
Prov. 20:19	A gossip tells secrets, so don't hang around with someone who talks too much.

Prov. 18:8   What dainty morsels rumors are – but they sink deep into one's heart.

23 – Always a willing worker

Prov. 12:11   Hard work means prosperity; only fools idle away their time.

Prov. 12:24   Work hard and become a leader; be lazy and become a slave.

Prov. 12:27   Lazy people don't even cook the game they catch, but the diligent makes use of everything they find.

Prov. 22:29   Do you see any truly competent workers? They will serve kings rather than ordinary people.

1 Thess. 4:11-12

This should be your ambition: to live a quiet life, minding your own business and working with your hands, just as we commanded you before. As a result, people who are not Christians will respect the way you live, and you will not need to depend on others to meet your financial needs.

1 Tim. 5:8   Those who won't care for their own relatives, especially those living in the same household, have denied what we believe. Such people are worse than unbelievers.

2 Thess. 3:10 Even while we were with you, we gave you this rule: "Whoever does not work should not eat."

24 – Working on developing all Fruit of the Spirit

Gal. 5:22-23   But when the Holy Spirit controls our lives, he will produce this kind of fruit in us: love, joy, peace, patience, kindness, goodness, faithfulness, gentleness, and self-control. Here there is no conflict with the law.

Psalm 64:10   The godly will rejoice in the Lord and find shelter in him. And those who do what is right will praise him.

Rom. 5:1   Since we have been made right in God's sight by faith, we have peace with God because of what Jesus Christ our Lord has done for us.

Prov. 16:32   It is better to be patient than powerful; it is better to have self-control than to conquer a city.

1 Peter 3:8   All of you should be of one mind, full of sympathy toward each other, loving one another with tender hearts and humble minds.

1 Peter 3:3-4 Don't be concerned about the outward beauty that depends on fancy hairstyles, expensive jewelry, or beautiful clothes. You should be known for the beauty that comes from within, the unfading beauty of a gentle and quiet spirit, which is so precious to God.

1 Cor. 13:4-7 Love is patient and kind. Love is not jealous or boastful or proud or rude. Love does not demand its own way. Love is not irritable, and it keeps no record of when it has been wronged. It is never glad about injustice but rejoices whenever the truth wins out. Love never gives up, never loses faith, is always hopeful, and endures through every circumstance.

25 – Hate sin – run, not tiptoe away from it

Jer. 17:9-10   The human heart is most deceitful and desperately wicked. Who really knows how bad it is? But I know! I, the Lord, search all hearts and examine secret motives. I give all people their due rewards, according to what their actions deserve.

Psalm 51:1-2, 10

               Have mercy on me, O God, because of your unfailing love. Because of your great compassion, blot out the stain of my sins. Wash me clean from my guilt. Purify me from my sin. Create in me a clean heart, O God. Renew a right spirit within me.

Rom. 6:6   Our old sinful selves were crucified with Christ so that sin might lose its power in our lives. We are no longer slaves to sin.

1 John 1:7   If we are living in the light of God's presence, just as Christ is, then we have fellowship with each other, and the blood of Jesus, his Son, cleanses us from every sin.

James 5:16   Confess your sins to each other and pray for each other so that you may be healed. The earnest prayer of a righteous person has great power and wonderful results.

Prov. 28:13   People who cover over their sins will not prosper. But if they confess and forsake them, they will receive mercy.

Psalm 32:1-2   O, what joy for those whose rebellion is forgiven, whose sin is put out of sight! Yes, what joy for those who record the Lord has cleared of sin, whose lives are lived in complete honesty!

26 – Primary goal is to see souls saved and stay saved

Amos 5:21-24   I hate all your show and pretense – the hypocrisy of your religious festivals and solemn assemblies. I will not accept your burnt offerings and grain offerings. I won't even notice all your choice peace offerings. Away with your hymns of praise! They are only noise to my ears. I will not listen to your music, no matter how lovely it is. Instead, I want to see a mighty flood of justice, a river of righteousness living that will never run dry.

Acts 1:16   For I am not ashamed of the gospel of Christ, for it is the power of God to salvation for everyone who believes, for the Jew first and also for the Greek.

Matt. 10:32-33 Therefore, whoever confesses Me before men, him I will also confess before My Father who is in heaven. But whoever denies Me before men, him I will also deny before My Father who is in heaven.

Acts 2:38   Then Peter said to them, "Repent and let every one of you be baptized in the name of Jesus Christ for the remission of sins; and you shall receive the gift of the Holy Spirit.

Acts 5:27-29   And when they had brought them, they set them before the council. And the high priest asked them, saying, "Did we not strictly command you not to teach in this name? And look, you have filled Jerusalem with your doctrine, and intend to bring this Man's blood on us!" But Peter and the other apostles answered and said: "We ought to obey God rather than men."

Acts 8:5-6   Then Philip went down to the city of Samaria and preached Christ to them. And the multitudes with one accord heeded the things spoken by Philip, hearing and seeing the miracles when he did.

Acts 14:21-22   And when they had preached the gospel to that city and made many disciples, they returned to Lystra, Iconium, and Antioch, strengthening the souls of the disciples, exhorting them to continue in the faith, and saying, "We must through many tribulations enter the kingdom of God.

27 – Don't backstab – seek to remove the knife and heal the wound

Prov. 10:12   Hatred stirs up quarrels, but love covers all offenses.

Prov. 15:1   A gentle answer turns away wrath, but harsh words stir up anger.

Prov. 28:25   Greed causes fighting; trusting the Lord leads to prosperity.

1 Cor. 3:3   You are still controlled by your own sinful desires. You are jealous of one another and quarrel with each other. Doesn't that prove you are controlled by your own desires? You are acting like people who don't belong to the Lord.

2 Tim. 2:14,16   Remind everyone of these things, and command them in God's name to stop fighting over words. Such arguments are useless, and they can ruin those who hear them. Avoid godless, foolish discussions that lead to more and more ungodliness.

1 Cor. 6:1-2   When you have something against another Christian, why do you file a lawsuit and ask a secular court to decide the matter, instead of taking it to other Christians to decide who is right? Don't you know that someday we Christians are going to judge the world?

Prov. 20:3   Avoiding a fight is a mark of honor; only fools insist on quarreling.

28 – Have a meek and humble spirit

Matt. 5:5   God blesses those who are gentle and lowly, for the whole earth will belong to them.

Psalm 149:4   The Lord delights in his people; he crowns the humble with salvation.

Zeph. 2:3   Beg the Lord to save you – all you who are humble, all you who uphold justice. Walk humbly and do what is right. Perhaps even yet the Lord will protect you from his anger on that day of destruction.

Ephes. 4:2   Be humble and gentle. Be patient with each other, making allowance for each other's faults because of your love.

Isaiah 29:19   The humble will be filled with fresh joy from the Lord. Those who are poor will rejoice in the Holy One of Israel.

Psalm 25:9   He leads the humble in what is right, teaching them his way.

Col. 3:12-14   Since God chose you to be the holy people whom he loves, you must clothe yourselves with tenderhearted mercy, kindness, humility, gentleness, and patience. You must make allowance for each other's faults and forgive the person who offends you. Remember, the Lord forgave you, so you must forgive others. And the most important piece of clothing you must wear is love. Love is what binds us all together in perfect harmony.

29 – Praise and worship God in spirit and in truth

Lev. 26:11-12   I will live among you, and I will not despise you. I will walk among you; I will be your God, and you will be my people.

Matt. 18:20   Where two or three gather together because they are mine, I am there among them.

Ps. 149:1   Praise ye the Lord. Sing unto the Lord a new song, and praise in the congregation of saints.

1 Thess. 5:18   In everything give thanks: for this is the will of God in Christ Jesus concerning you.

Heb. 13:15   By Him therefore let us offer the sacrifice of praise to God continually, that is, the fruit of our lips giving thanks to His name.

Acts 1:8   When the Holy Spirit comes upon you, you will receive power and will tell people about me everywhere – in Jerusalem, throughout Judea, in Samaria, and to the ends of the earth.

John 16:13-15 When the Spirit of truth comes, he will guide you into all truth. He will not be presenting his own ideas; he will be telling you what he has heard. He will tell you about the future. He will bring me glory by revealing to you whatever he receives from me. All that the Father has is mine; this is what I mean when I say that the Spirit will reveal to you whatever he receives from me.

30 – Saved, filled with the Holy Ghost

There is no middle of the road, either you are saved and filled with the Holy Ghost or you are not. Read Acts, Chapters 1 and 2.

Notes & Reflections

Notes & Reflections (cont'd)

Notes & Reflections (cont'd)

About The Author

Dr. Elizabeth A. James (E.A. James) has been writing for over 40 years. She is a licensed and ordained minister and has been President and Founder of Fast And Indispensable Temporary Help (F.A.I.T.H.) Ministries, Inc. since February, 1999. She is also the Editor-in-Chief of FM Publishing Company (2009) and Senior Managing Director of Geri Lorraine Enterprises, LLC (2000). In 2014, she became a supplier, independent marketer, and supporter with TAG Team Marketing International and a dedicated member of the Black Business Network.

After attending over 10 colleges, she has a doctorate in Theology & Biblical Counseling, a master's in Education, bachelor's degree in English, and major course work in subjects such as Business Management, Biomedical Engineering, Pre-Med, and Chemistry.

In addition to many other accomplishments, E.A. James has received the Woman of Excellence Award, is a member of the blackwritersconnect.com, and has won several awards for her poetry. She is currently a business consultant, certified teacher, and Nationally-Certified Manager of Program Improvement.

Titles by E.A. James:

Spiritual Cosmetics for the Soul (devotionals)
The Last Visitor (historical fiction)
Being a Well Body of Believers (nonfiction)
This Hill I Climb (poetry)
The Reason Why I Sing (poetry/songs)
Driving Tips for BOOHs (Bats Out of Hell) (satire)
7-Day Emergency Help for OWIACs (Of Whom I Am Chief) (devotionals)
Why I Should Hate Men, But Don't (nonfiction)
Will Work for Food, Family & Freedom (nonfiction)
Casino Con: An Eye-Opening Look From the Inside Out (nonfiction)

Publication and Catalog Ordering Information

To order books by E.A. James or to inquire about screenplay production rights:

Order online at: www.fmpublishingcompany.com

Email: fmpublishing@cox.net

Fax: 800-518-1219

FM Publishing Co.

www.ingramcontent.com/pod-product-compliance
Lightning Source LLC
Chambersburg PA
CBHW071343090426
42738CB00012B/2997